CELEBRATING
GOOD
LITURGY

A Guide to the Ministries of the Mass

Edited by JAMES MARTIN, SJ

LOYOLAPRESS.

CHICAGO

LoyolaPress.

3441 N. Ashland Avenue
Chicago, Illinois 60657
(800) 621-1008
www.loyolabooks.org

Cover photograph: Catholic News Service

Cover and interior design by Arc Group Ltd.

Library of Congress Cataloging-in-Publication Data
Celebrating good liturgy : a guide to the ministries of the Mass   /
edited by James Martin.
        p.   cm.
    ISBN 0-8294-2119-X
    1.   Mass.   I.   Martin, James. S.J.
BX2230.3.C42   2005
264'.0203—dc22

                                        2004028747

Printed in the United States of America
05 06 07 08 09 10 Versa 10 9 8 7 6 5 4 3 2 1

To the worshiping communities at

Epiphany of Our Lord Catholic Church,
Plymouth Meeting, Pennsylvania

St. Agatha-St. James Church,
Philadelphia, Pennsylvania

St. Vincent Ferrer Church,
New York, New York

St. Leo Parish,
Stamford, Connecticut

Blessed Sacrament Church,
Jamaica Plain, Massachusetts

Madonna della Strada Chapel,
Chicago, Illinois

St. Joseph the Worker Church,
Nairobi, Kenya

St. Peter Parish,
Cambridge, Massachusetts

The Church of St. Ignatius Loyola,
New York, New York,

who have helped me to understand
what it means to "celebrate" the Mass.

Do this in remembrance of me.

LUKE 22:19

CONTENTS

❀ Introduction ❀

James Martin, SJ

How many debates have you heard about the way that Mass is celebrated in your parish?

Few discussions can animate (and agitate) American Catholics more than those over liturgical topics. In other words, if you want a lively discussion in your parish, just bring up any of the following topics: the use of inclusive language, the selection of hymns, the quality (and length) of the homily, whether to kneel at the consecration, the role of eucharistic ministers, the perceived degree of "reverence" among the congregation, who shakes hands and who doesn't at the sign of peace, and how closely the presider follows the prescribed rubrics.

When carried out in a parish community with trust, such conversations can lead to improvements in parish life and a deepening of appreciation of the Mass. Just as often, however, they can devolve into what are known as "liturgy wars," leading to frustration and even anger. Too often, the "sacrament of unity" can be a source of disunity in parishes.

Unfortunately, such "liturgy wars" can distract Catholics from what they care most about—the Eucharist, the sacrament described by the Second Vatican Council as "the true center of the whole Christian life for the universal church and the local congregation."

In an attempt to refresh Catholics on the subject of the liturgy, *America,* the national Catholic magazine, recently offered its readers a multipart series entitled Good Liturgy. This book gathers together all those essays, which proved popular with readers, especially pastors and pastoral teams across the country. After the initial series appeared, the magazine received dozens of requests for reprints—a more or less infallible indication of the usefulness of a particular article.

In the following chapters, some of the country's leading liturgical scholars, experts, and practitioners consider the liturgy from the vantage point of the variety of "roles" of the participants in the Mass. They examine how each participant can more fully contribute to the celebration of "good liturgy" in the church today.

You might be curious about the structure of the book. Why focus on the roles that make up the celebration of the liturgy? Why not focus, for instance, on the structure of the Mass itself—for example, one essay on the introductory rite, one on the readings, one on the Eucharistic Prayers, and so on? That was certainly one possibility. But in the end, it seemed better to focus on something both more specific and more practical: the individual contributions that each person makes to the Eucharist, in order to offer people a better sense of how they could participate fully and actively in the Mass. Not only would this enable persons serving in these ministries to reflect on their own roles, it also would enable Catholics to better understand what the other person is doing. In other words, I imagine a deacon might say, "Now I better understand what our ministers of hospitality really do," or a eucharistic minister saying, "Now I finally see why the music ministers are so important."

Our essays begin with the assembly, the role in which the vast majority of Catholics find themselves during the celebration of the Eucharist. Indeed, the assembly is seen at the heart of all the ministries in the book: presiders, deacons, lectors, eucharistic ministers, music ministers, parish liturgical councils, and ministers of hospitality. All these ministries are viewed, essentially, as serving the assembly. The final essay, by Nathan D. Mitchell, associate director of the Center for Pastoral Liturgy at the University of Notre Dame, is a sort of drawing together of the previous chapters and also offers a short list of what makes for a "good liturgy."

The essayists were asked to take a broad look at each role in order to situate the particular ministry: its underlying spirituality and theology, as well as its history, current questions about its place in the Mass, helpful practices, and also practical examples from personal experience. Though our writers are experts in the field and often teach liturgical theology in colleges and universities, I asked them to avoid a purely academic approach and, instead, to speak more personally to readers.

You'll notice that our writers make ample use of Scripture, historical documents, and recent Vatican teachings. At the same time, the contributors were asked not to focus too much on the hot-button topics that have bogged down liturgical scholars and experts during the past few decades. So while some essays mention these disputes (for example, when does the eucharistic minister receive Communion?), they center more on the basics of the individual ministries.

As an aside, you don't have to be a liturgical scholar or an expert in liturgical practices to appreciate these essays. (I am certainly neither of those things.) A few things, though, are helpful to know from the outset.

First of all, nearly all the essayists refer to a document called Sacrosanctum Concilium. This was the first major publication of the Second Vatican Council and was issued on December 4, 1963. Vatican documents usually take their names from their first two words. Sacrosanctum Concilium really means "This Sacred Council," but it is often referred to by its official English title, "Constitution on the Sacred Liturgy." (Sometimes the essayists simply use the shorthand S.C.)

One of the most well-known writings of the Council, Sacrosanctum Concilium set in motion the grand liturgical reforms that were a hallmark of Vatican II. Besides reminding Catholics that the liturgy is the central act of worship in the church, S.C. called for "full, conscious, and active" participation by the laity during the Mass. The document inspired a host of reforms that revolutionized the liturgy, most famously in its desire for clarified and simplified rituals, and especially, the call for the Mass to be celebrated in "vernacular" or local languages. Indeed, if you ask most American Catholics what Vatican II did, the first answer you'll probably hear is, "It changed the Mass from Latin to English." That's primarily the work of Sacrosanctum Concilium.

Like many Council documents, Sacrosanctum Concilium not only laid the foundations for eventual reforms of the church but also makes for inspiring reading in its own right. At the end of this book are some of the more important passages from S.C. I hope that these brief selections from this great work of the Council will help deepen your understanding of the essays, as well as provide you with some beautiful passages for personal prayer and reflection.

Another document frequently referred to in this book is the General Instruction of the Roman Missal, also referred to by the rather infelicitous acronym G.I.R.M. This was a document on the celebration of the Mass published in 1969 by the Vatican's Sacred

Congregation of Divine Worship. The General Instruction was intended as part of the new Roman Missal promulgated by Pope Paul VI. Essentially, it addressed the specific ways and practices that are required for the celebration of the Mass, a kind of how-to manual of liturgical practices. In 1975, it was slightly altered; and then, in 2002, a new document, the Revised General Instruction of the Roman Missal, was issued.

Now a bit of a personal note. Part of the fun of collecting and editing these essays was not only revisiting some topics I first encountered during my theology studies, but also discovering some brand-new ideas and insights. Frankly, it never dawned on me until I read Keith Pecklers's essay on presiding that one reason that it's preferable not to speak aloud all the celebrant's prayers is that a little silence is not such a bad idea. For another thing, I hadn't really thought of hospitality as "everyone's ministry" until I read Thomas Richstatter's reflections. And then I thought, *Of course.* And until I read Kathy Lindell's chapter on the parish liturgical committee, I never imagined what kinds of challenges and difficulties such groups could face.

After collecting and editing these essays, I noticed that not only did I celebrate Mass a little differently (and better, I hope!) but also that, to paraphrase Vatican II, I more fully and actively understood the value of everyone's ministry. All of this added to my appreciation of the church's great sacrament.

Overall, I hope that this book will prove helpful to all members of the worshiping community—clergy and laypersons alike—and serve as a reminder that, in the words of Sacrosanctum Concilium, the church everywhere "seeks continually to understand and to live the Eucharist more fully."

James Martin, SJ
July 31, 2005
Feast of St. Ignatius Loyola

❀ The Assembly ❀

Robert D. Duggan

The Reverend Robert D. Duggan is pastor of St. Rose of Lima Parish in Gaithersburg, Maryland, and is a columnist for Church magazine.

One of the most important pastoral challenges I have faced as a parish priest over the past thirty years has been helping the faithful overcome a legacy of passivity and the notion that it's "Father's Mass, not ours."

Certainly progress has been made since the Second Vatican Council, but a survey of the current liturgical landscape reveals mixed results. Catholics have a solid, well-articulated theology of the assembly's role at the Eucharist, a vision backed by numerous official pronouncements stretching back to Pius X in the early twentieth century. But many people in the pews are unaware of that theology. And they continue to struggle with a deeply entrenched clericalism and disenfranchisement of the laity at Mass, conditions passed on from generation to generation through subtle attitudes and behaviors that continue to communicate the message that it really is "Father's Mass."

Still, more and more among the laity are beginning to make connections between their dignity as baptized persons and their responsibility to participate actively in the Eucharist. The ongoing work of liturgical renewal has made many inroads, developing an awareness of the importance of the assembly's role at worship and teaching a variety of practical skills that enable fuller participation. Nonetheless, old habits die hard, and practices still taken for granted in many parishes militate against real ownership of the liturgical action by the assembly at large.

The Assembly Since Vatican II

If history is ultimately to judge the Spirit-led *aggiornamento,* or "updating," called for by Pope John XXIII a success, it will in no small measure be the result of the people of God awakening to the privileges and responsibilities that are theirs by virtue of baptism.

Nowhere is this more obvious than in the Second Vatican Council's renewal of the liturgy, now a work forty years in progress but truly just beginning in earnest. The hierarchical church has done its work reasonably well—despite some signs of retrenchment in recent years—by publishing an entire corpus of revised liturgical books, enacting enough rubrics and liturgical laws to fill a small library and overseeing the process of translation and inculturation with watchful, if somewhat timorous, eyes. What remains to be accomplished is mostly at the local level, where the people of God gather on Sunday mornings to face the challenge of breathing life into the liturgy, turning "correct" liturgical forms into true celebrations of faith.

Much has been said since the Council about what must be done to renew the various ministries that collaborate in the Eucharist. But the foundation for all ecclesial renewal, and for a renewed liturgical experience in particular, rests with a faith-filled, well-informed, and committed assembly of the faithful who do their job with the "full, conscious, and active participation"

(Sacrosanctum Concilium, No. 14) that is rightly theirs by virtue of their baptismal consecration as a royal priesthood.

Since Vatican II, there has been no lack of official documents that emphasize the importance of the ministry of the liturgical assembly. The General Instruction of the Roman Missal says that at Mass the people of God "offer the spotless Victim not only through the hands of the priest, but also together with him . . ." (No. 95). Another recent document from the Vatican—entitled "Directory on Popular Piety and the Liturgy" and released in 2002—minces no words in describing how historical factors during the Middle Ages and afterward resulted in a passive, non-participatory role for the faithful at Mass, a problem we are still working to overcome. The directory points out that one cause of this lamentable development was "a weakening of a sense of the universal priesthood in virtue of which the faithful offer 'spiritual sacrifices pleasing to God, through Jesus Christ' (1 Pt 2:5; Rm 12:1), and, according to their condition, participate fully in the church's worship" (No. 48).

Today, the impact of these official documents needs to become part of the awareness of the assembly at large. It is they—just as much as the presider—who must offer the great sacrifice of praise and thanksgiving to God. It is they—just as much as the presider—who carry responsibility to say the prayers and sing the songs prescribed for them in the ritual texts. It is they—just as much as the presider—who must be channels of the Spirit's consecratory power, allowing the gift of themselves to be transformed as surely as the gifts of bread and wine are changed into Christ's body and blood.

For nearly two decades, I have been blessed to minister as pastor in a parish community that takes seriously its responsibility for eucharistic celebrations that are vibrant and faith filled. Without wishing to suggest that we have "arrived" or are a "model" parish (we haven't and we aren't), nonetheless, I have experienced firsthand some of what it takes to restore to the assembly its sense of ownership of the liturgical action. Realizing that others may wish to add to my list, I offer my own formula for success in helping the assembly achieve that "full, conscious, and active participation" at the Sunday Eucharist of which the official documents speak.

- *Help the entire assembly find its voice in singing at the Eucharist.* As long as large numbers of Catholics remain mute when the liturgy calls for the assembly to sing, true liturgical renewal will elude us. No single element will make as much difference as the empowerment of the faithful. We still need a better repertoire, better training, better song leaders, and a shared conviction that song is an essential way for us to lift our voices in prayer as a community of the redeemed. But when all those pieces fall into place, the assembly experiences the power of its prayer in a way that, as one of my parishioners said, "knocks their socks off."

- *Proclaim and preach the Scriptures in a way that engages at a deep level the attention (and faith) of the assembly.* There is no more profound experience of communal participation in the liturgy than the utter stillness that overtakes a community that has just heard the word of God proclaimed (or preached) with a power that takes the breath away. Lectors and homilists carry a heavy burden if they are to reach that degree of effectiveness on a regular basis. But members of the faithful also share responsibility for becoming more scripturally literate and for demanding a higher-quality experience from those who minister the word to them on Sunday morning.

- *Rework the choreography of the Eucharistic Prayer in order to engage the assembly more actively in its proclamation.* This will require more refined skills by presiders who proclaim the text, a more interactive structure (like the sung acclamations that punctuate the children's Eucharistic Prayers), and a more coherent "body language" that allows for a single posture (preferably standing along with the presider) from start to finish. Most critically it requires—on the part of the faithful—a more highly developed interior awareness of offering themselves, along with the presider, in the great sacrifice of thanksgiving and praise that is the Eucharistic Prayer.

- *Address issues of ecclesiology and Christian identity as the backdrop against which full and active participation makes sense.* The people of God require a lived experience that "We are the church." In order for this to happen, many other aspects of church governance and polity will have to be considerably different from their present experience. In addition, membership and belonging must be defined in terms of a faith that is deliberately chosen and consciously lived (as it is presently, for example, in the adult-initiation process). This kind of faith must characterize the assembly at large. Moreover, conversion to discipleship—not mere cultural Catholicism—must be the normative understanding of our Christian identity. It would be wonderful if the hierarchy were to take the lead in this regard, but the parish is where people live their lives. Nothing prevents local communities from offering their members right now a practical "ecclesiology of belonging" to meet these needs.

- *Implement regularly the full range of ritual options that already help the assembly's active participation, and keep an eye open for others that might yet be developed.* A good example of this is the adult-initiation model, which stresses the ritual involvement of the entire community in the "work" of making new Christians. This requires of the assembly a willingness to be "stretched" in its ritual repertoire of gestures, processions, and other elements that call for the engagement of their bodies, as well as their minds and hearts. Ordinary Catholics need to know in their bones that their full participation in the ritual action is crucial for its success. You will know this is working when more people arrive on time and fewer leave early!

- *Promote as the context for the Eucharist a gathering that is warm and friendly, welcoming of diversity and hospitable to the stranger.* We can no longer tolerate the perception that parishes where the worship is more relaxed and friendly are "Protestant" in style. The call to be evangelizing communities requires that the "frozen chosen" thaw out and show in real, human terms—above all, when they gather for worship—the joy that befits a community claiming to know in a personal way the saving grace of Jesus Christ. The isolationism seen in the privatized, individualistic way so many Catholics still worship must give way to a more highly developed awareness that the eucharistic liturgy is public and communal by nature, the "work" of the entire people of God united in a single prayer of praise and thanksgiving.

- *Continue to teach, reflect on, and preach about the importance of baptism and its intimate connection with the offering of the eucharistic sacrifice.* Catholics need to have a strongly developed liturgical spirituality that makes them more aware that at the Eucharist they join with the presider in the offering that Christ, the one and only high priest, makes to his Father for the life of the world. The royal priesthood of baptism consecrates the assembly of believers to a life of worship that finds its "source and summit" in the eucharistic gathering, and the faithful deserve to know about the solid theology that supports this perspective.

- *Recognize that the assembly's full participation in the Eucharist requires as a normative practice Communion under both kinds from elements consecrated at that liturgy.* Denying the cup to the entire assembly and serving "leftovers" consecrated at a previous celebration are vestiges of a pre-Vatican II practice and strike at the heart of the assembly's full participation in the Eucharist. The faithful who still do not value the importance of partaking of both bread and wine consecrated at this particular sacred meal need to be helped to gain that appreciation. The complicitous silence of the faithful as their bishops solve the priest shortage with "Sunday Communion Services in the Absence of a Priest" is symptomatic of a failure to claim their right to the celebration of the Sunday Eucharist as baptized members of the Body of Christ. That such a solution is spreading so quickly (and with so little protest) indicates how much work remains to be done among the people of God in order to reclaim the vision described so glowingly by Pope John Paul II in his apostolic letter "On Keeping the Lord's Day Holy" (Dies Domini).

Personal experience has taught me that these steps are not only important, but also achievable. The Council's call for a renewed liturgy—celebrated by assemblies that participate fully, consciously, and actively in the Sunday Eucharist—is not the idle fantasy of starry-eyed idealists. Rather, it is the inspired vision of Spirit-led leaders, who dared to dream of a renewed church, gathered around the table of the Lord, singing God's praise with all the gusto of true believers.

Presiding at the Liturgy of the Word

John F. Baldovin, SJ

John F. Baldovin, SJ, teaches historical and liturgical theology at the Weston Jesuit School of Theology, Cambridge, Massachusetts. Father Baldovin's newest book is Bread of Life, Cup of Salvation: Understanding the Mass.

There is a saying, "Well begun is half done." Liturgical celebrations are among the places where that is especially true. What follows is one presider's and teacher's reflection on the first half of the liturgy of the Mass, from before the entrance procession to the end of the Prayer of the Faithful. The basic principle here is that the role of the priest-presider, or celebrant of the Eucharist, is to serve and encourage the prayer of the assembly that God has gathered in a particular place, so that they can give praise to God and grow in their response to the gift of Christ in word and sacrament.

The tone of the liturgy is set by the presider at the very beginning. After some comments on the history, theology, and spirituality of the Liturgy of the Word, I will turn to some dos and don'ts of presiding, and conclude with some reflections on preaching.

A Very Brief History

As far as we can tell, during the first four centuries A.D., the Liturgy of the Word began with a liturgical greeting by the president of the assembly; then came the readings—and that was about it. St. Justin Martyr (writing about mid-second-century Rome) tells us that on Sundays, "[T]he memoirs of the apostles or the writings of the prophets are read, as much as there is time for. Then, when the reader has finished, the one presiding, provides, in a discourse, admonition and exhortation to imitate these excellent things. Then we all stand up together and say prayers. . . ."

In some of the early church communities, as many as four or five readings were proclaimed. By the Middle Ages, the Western church, with some rare exceptions, used two readings: one from the Gospels and another from Paul or some other New Testament book. Biblical chants (mostly psalms) always have been interspersed among the readings. As the chants became more elaborate, the texts were abbreviated, so that very few verses were sung. Another medieval development, probably an expansion of the alleluia verse, was the sequence hymn sung on special occasions— for example, "Sion, Praise Your Savior" on Corpus Christi, "Dies Irae" at Masses for the Dead, and "Praise the Paschal Victim" on Easter. The Gospel was traditionally chanted by a deacon. This is, as the General Instruction of the Roman Missal says, a ministerial, not a presidential function in the liturgy (No. 59). The Nicene Creed became a regular part of the Sunday Eucharist in the tenth century, imported from the Greek East. The Prayer of the Faithful disappeared after the beginning of the fifth century but has been restored in the post-Vatican II rite.

Theology and Spirituality

With what theology and spirituality can the presider approach this combination of rites that we call the Liturgy of the Word? A few principles from the General Instruction can help. First, the entrance rites should "ensure that the faithful who come together as one establish Communion and dispose themselves properly to God's word and to celebrate the Eucharist worthily" (No. 46). Second, the instruction emphasizes that in the proclamation of the word, God is speaking: Christ himself is present in our midst (Nos. 29, 55).

There are two spiritual implications that might inform the presider's approach to these basic aspects of the first part of the Mass: humility and reverence. If presiders are not awe-struck by the fact that Christ is really present in his word and that God is actually speaking to us, how can we expect anyone else to appreciate God's word as the most fundamental source of our faith? So the presider's task is to exercise a kind of enthusiastic humility (if that's not too much of an oxymoron) during the Liturgy of the Word.

Second, the instruction also affirms the presence of Christ in the midst of the gathered assembly (No. 27). This implies that the presider needs to show reverence not only for the liturgy but also for his fellow members of the Body of Christ, for whose leadership he has been called. The presider's role during the entrance rites and the Liturgy of the Word is a rather modest one. He leads by listening. The priest has a very delicate role in the liturgy: He represents Christ to the assembly (which is the Body of Christ), and he represents the body of Christ to God. In a sense, he is the quintessential middleman.

Pitfalls and Good Practices in Presiding

There are both opportunities and pitfalls for presiders, right from the beginning of the entrance rite to the end of the intercessions. The entire celebration can start off on the wrong foot when a cantor or commentator begins with something like, "Good morning; let's all stand and greet our celebrant, Father Jim, with the hymn . . ." I think (I hope) that everyone knows that the point of the opening song is not to greet the presider, but to gather the assembly to praise God and to hear God's word.

The liturgical scholar Ralph Keifer pointed out some time ago that there is an irony about the post-Vatican II liturgy. While today's liturgy balances the role of the priest and the assembly theologically, it seems to give more emphasis to the personality of the priest and so reverses that balance ritually. Given the danger that the liturgy can so easily be mistaken for entertainment (instead of a communal response to God's invitation), the presider needs to be very careful not to make himself the center of attention. There are several ways this can happen. The priest might add "Good morning" to the ritual greeting "The Lord be with you." I have heard priests respond, "Thank you" to the people's "And also with you." Or the priest can act as if he were host of the gathering in his introduction to the celebration: "I'm so happy you can be here today." I've heard even visiting priests do that. It is not for nothing that some have suggested that we have merely substituted a new, more informal, clericalism for the old one.

The Sacramentary and General Instruction both allow for the priest to offer a "very brief" introduction to the liturgy of the day in his own words immediately after the greeting. How is a new clericalism to be avoided here? One way is to think of this introduction as exhortation rather than information. It is not meant to be a summary or preview of the homily but a means of helping the assembly to praise God, to recognize their need for forgiveness, and to hear God's word.

I should also mention the practice of adding phrases like, "My brothers and sisters, the Lord be with you." During the course I teach to future priests on liturgical presiding, I ask, "How do those added words improve on what the church is offering in the liturgy?" I rarely hear a good answer. This is not liturgical nitpicking so much as a way to point out that the liturgy is a common possession of the people of God, not the property of the priest, however well-meaning he may be.

This leads to a larger issue: Is there a legitimate variety of liturgical styles? The answer is, quite simply, yes. The presider's style of introducing the liturgy may well differ among African-American, "Anglo," and Latino assemblies, since these varied groups may well need different approaches in order to gather in praise and be prepared to listen to the word of God. At the same time, we need to be wary of a simplistic equation of formality with a cold manner or stiffness. It seems to me that the best presiders combine respect for the assembly and ritual formality with great warmth and engagement—what I like to call "high-church-with-a-heart."

Let us turn to the penitential rite. The third form of the rite, which combines acclamations directed to Christ with the response "Lord [Christ], have mercy," has become the clear favorite in our celebrations. The priest (or deacon or cantor) may use the acclamations printed in the Sacramentary or others. Note, however, that when the directions say "using these or similar words," they mean that what is improvised should follow the form and intent of the examples given. First of all, then, these are acclamations addressed not to the persons of the Trinity but to Christ; second, they do not focus on our sins but on Christ and his activity ("You came to call sinners"). It is also good to remember that the rite of sprinkling is recommended on Sundays (especially in the Easter season) as a way of remembering our baptisms.

"Glory to God in the Highest" is a hymn that we sing every Sunday except in the seasons of Lent and Advent. It is the nature of a hymn to be sung. Many of our congregations have difficulty with singing, and sometimes this difficulty is exacerbated by the reluctance of their priests to sing. We certainly need to take much more seriously in our seminary education the training of priests to sing. The "Glory to God" is followed by the opening prayer, which brings a close to the entrance rites. This is one of the places where the re-emphasis on silence noted in the General Instruction is important. The priest says, "Let us pray." This invitation refers to the silence in which all who are gathered offer up their prayer. The technical name for what follows is the "collect": it sums up or collects the silent prayers of the assembled.

Can it be said that presiders do not need to be active during the proclamation of the word? It is clear that reading the Scriptures is a ministerial, not a presidential role. The presider is to cede the reading of the Gospel to a deacon or to a concelebrating priest, if there is one. I sympathize with priests who are going to preach and want to read the Gospel so that they can give it their own emphasis, but this value does not outrank the importance of respecting the liturgy as a combination of coordinated roles imaging the body of Christ.

On the other hand, even when the presider is not speaking, he should be an active hearer of the word. If the presider does not have his eyes on the reader or otherwise show that he is listening attentively, the rest of the assembly receives a subtle but nonetheless clear signal that it is not important for them to listen either. What would change in our liturgies if we all believed that the word of God is a matter of life and death? After all, it is.

Proclaiming the Word

There are four ways in which we respond to the proclamation of God's word: the homily, the Creed, the Prayer of the Faithful, and the Eucharistic Prayer and Communion. Preaching is obviously the most important thing presiders do during the Liturgy of the Word. Presuming the presider's strong and living faith, I offer here only three points on something that deserves a much longer reflection. First, it is important to remember that the liturgical homily is a way to connect a particular assembly's experience with God's living word. Second, this means that the preacher must have a good "feel" for each assembly. He is not merely offering an exegesis or explanation of the Scriptures—although that prior work needs to be done in his office and in his prayer. Third, there is no substitute for being an interesting person. Preachers need to read (fiction, nonfiction, and poetry); they need to go to movies and concerts, and watch television; they need to listen to music of many sorts. In other words, they need to be thoroughly engaged both in reflection on Scripture and theology, and in the culture in which they live. They should have something significant to say.

On Sundays and major feast days we proclaim the Creed. The newest edition of the texts for the Mass gives the option of using either the Nicene or the (much shorter) Apostles' Creed. Creeds are not so much a series of statements giving information about God as they are a way of expressing the grammar of faith and a means of praise. (We also need good and relatively easy melodies so that the creeds can be sung more often.)

The final element in the Liturgy of the Word is the Prayer of the Faithful. Once again, the presider's role is modest but significant. He introduces the petitions by an invitation to pray. (Note that the invitation is not itself a prayer.) As mentioned earlier with regard to reading the Gospel, the Roman Catholic liturgy is a "team sport" and calls for a reader, cantor, or deacon to read the petitions. The presider then concludes the prayer by speaking a formula, examples of which are given in appendix 1 of the Sacramentary. Published sets of original prayers composed with the readings of the Lectionary in mind may also be useful.

Together with Christ

I have been using the word *presider,* in addition to the terms used by the General Instruction, *priest* or *priest-celebrant.* I have adopted this terminology deliberately. In a real sense, the entire assembly is the celebrant of the liturgy together with Christ, whose Spirit calls it into being. The presider's role is both critical and limited.

He is given the noble task of symbolizing the community's unity and calling it to worship the Lord of all. That is no small grace, but a wonderful privilege.

The revised edition of the General Instruction of the Roman Missal provides us all, clergy and laypeople alike, with a golden opportunity to reflect on the importance of carefully preparing and engaging in our eucharistic celebrations. May that reflection deepen our worship and response to the God who never ceases to call us to deeper and richer life.

Presiding
※ at the Liturgy ※
of the Eucharist

Keith F. Pecklers, SJ

Keith F. Pecklers, SJ, is professor of liturgy at the Pontifical Gregorian University in Rome and professor of liturgical history at the Pontifical Liturgical Institute of San Anselmo. Father Peckler's recent books include Dynamic Equivalence: The Living Language of Christian Worship; Worship: A Primer in Christian Ritual; *and an edited volume,* Liturgy in a Postmodern World.

By the sixteenth century, the priest had become such a predominant figure in the celebration of Mass that several bishops at the Council of Trent (1545–64) went on record with a startling proposal. Perhaps it would be better, they suggested, if the laity just stayed at home and let the priest say his Mass without the distraction of a congregation.

This breathtaking idea was rejected, but it showed how far the eucharistic liturgy had strayed from the assemblies of the early church, where the priest and people usually acted in tandem.

In fact, the church had to wait until the Second Vatican Council, some four hundred years later, before laypersons could regain their rightful place in the eucharistic liturgy. Today, the liturgy has come full circle, with the restoration of full and active participation for the whole church, and the recovery of the diversity of liturgical ministries. The priest has become the presider, who serves at the altar, first and foremost, as a member of the assembly, while still acting as both a representative of Christ *(in persona Christi)* and in the name of the church *(in persona ecclesiae).*

A Brief History: From Justin Martyr to Vatican II

In the early church there was a close link between presiding at the Eucharist and presidency over the local community's outreach to the poor and needy. The same person who stood at the altar to proclaim the Eucharistic Prayer also looked after the material needs of the community. As noted in the classic text of Justin Martyr (writing about mid-second-century Rome) in which a description of the Sunday Eucharist is presented, he mentions that a collection is taken at the end of the celebration, just before the deacons and deaconesses leave to bring Communion to the sick and homebound. The proceeds from the collection are given to the presider, who then sees that they are properly distributed to those in need. Justin provides a list of worthy recipients: orphans, widows, the sick, the incarcerated, foreigners, and anyone else who is in need.

Even today, the purpose of the collection that takes place at the preparation of the gifts is first of all for the needs of the poor, as the General Instruction says (No. 73). This reminds us of the important link between liturgy and social justice, and of the responsibility of the presider at the eucharistic table to embody that important relationship in his liturgical service of the assembly.

The Eucharistic Prayer lies at the heart of the entire liturgical celebration, the "source and summit of the liturgical action" (No. 78). In the early church the prayer was improvised; there were as yet no liturgical books. Justin Martyr reported that the prayer should be prayed to the best of the president's ability. (Apparently, all were not equally gifted in the craft of poetic improvisation.) Most significantly, the prayer was prayed as a single unified prayer. From start to finish, the presider proclaimed the Great

Thanksgiving with arms outstretched, while the whole assembly stood together around the altar singing its great Amen at the conclusion, expressing full assent to what was proclaimed.

In the medieval period, as the liturgy became increasingly clericalized, the distance between worship and daily life grew ever greater. The use of Latin perpetuated this distance, leaving the liturgy unintelligible to most. Mass also came to be celebrated facing the East, with the priest's back to the people. The Eucharistic Prayer was prayed silently by the priest, which underlined both its sacral nature and the belief that it no longer needed to involve the assembly directly. The prayer thus became divided, with the moment of consecration emphasized as the single most important moment in the whole Mass. (A bell was rung to alert the faithful that the moment had arrived.) The congregation no longer stood but knelt. Private Masses abounded.

In the twelfth century, chantry priests in England and elsewhere celebrated Masses throughout the day to keep pace with the demand. The focus was now on the "fruits of the Mass," which were applied to the living or the dead according to the priest's intention. Later, the Council of Trent's emphasis on rubrics brought new burdens to some priests who were already overly scrupulous. Fearful that they had pronounced the words of consecration improperly, some priests would repeat them over and over until they felt they had spoken them correctly.

The moment of Communion traditionally represented the fullness of unity in the one body of Christ and the commitment of believers to be broken as Christ's body and poured out as his blood. Accordingly, in the early church the chalice was always offered to communicants, as it was the most complete response to Jesus' command, "Take and eat, take and drink." But consistent with the overall decline in lay liturgical participation in the Middle Ages, all this later changed. Communion was no longer distributed during Mass, although this was sometimes done before or after Mass. And by the thirteenth century, the chalice was no longer offered to the laity. At the Council of Trent, there was some discussion in favor of offering the chalice to the laity, and permission was given for the practice in certain regions (e.g., Prague in the late sixteenth century), but the universal practice of making the chalice available to the laity would return only with the reforms of the Second Vatican Council.

The Dynamics of the Liturgy

The presider's principal role clearly emerges as the liturgy shifts from the ambo, where the word is proclaimed and preached, to the altar, which the church from its earliest days has revered as a primary symbol of Christ. For this reason, the presider reverences it with a profound bow and a kiss, and circles it with incense. It is also why, as noted in the General Instruction (No. 306), the altar is to remain uncluttered during the Liturgy of the Word except for the book of the Gospels, which is placed upon it. Likewise, during the Liturgy of the Eucharist, the altar should hold only those elements necessary for the celebration: bread, wine, chalice, and the Sacramentary or Missal. The General Instruction (No. 72) delineates three distinct parts of this rite: the preparation of the gifts, the Eucharistic Prayer, and, finally, the breaking of the bread and Communion of the faithful.

Members of the assembly take an active role in bringing forward the bread and wine in procession at the preparation of the gifts, sometimes preceded by the collection of monetary offerings, which are placed nearby. A profound bow to those who present the gifts can be one way for the presider to acknowledge both the gift and the giver. But sometimes I have seen the occasional smile, handshake, or kiss as the presider whispers, "Hey, thanks, Jennie. Thanks, Bob." Such gestures—made with the best of intentions, of course—easily personalize the exchange, but they also suggest that the gifts are somehow for the priest himself. This is one of those occasions where the presider can easily get in the way without intending to.

A similar dynamic can be observed during the preparation of the altar itself. The altar belongs to the whole assembly: Christ's mystical body. At the preparation, and even more during the Eucharistic Prayer, the presider should avoid giving the impression that it is his table or that the gifts being offered are his. When I am presiding, for example, I prefer that the gifts be placed squarely in the middle of the altar rather than nearest to where I stand. This is one small way of suggesting that the gifts of God belong to the people of God, as St. Augustine affirmed in the fourth century. The Sacramentary is then placed directly in front of where I stand. It is also preferable that someone other than the presider prepare the altar. If there is a deacon present, this is one of his responsibilities. On other occasions, the servers or other members of the assembly should do that task.

With the exception of the presentation of the gifts, the preparation is largely a passive time for the assembly and need not be drawn out or accentuated. When music is sung or instrumental music played, the presider is to say the preparatory prayers silently. When there is no music, he may say them either silently or aloud. As an antidote to the abundance of words in our reformed liturgy, I prefer to pray the preparatory prayers silently, but this is very much a matter of personal choice.

There is no option, however, for the presider to pray aloud the specifically private and silent prayers of the priest. Those prayers include the text that accompanies the washing of the hands, "Lord wash away my iniquity; cleanse me from my sin," and the preparatory prayers before Communion. They are prayed silently precisely because they are private. They belong to the personal piety and spirituality of the priest, and have no reference to the assembly. Since the liturgy is already sufficiently verbose, the rubric requiring silence here shows wisdom.

After the exchange "Pray, brothers and sisters" and the prayer over the gifts, the presider enters into the preface dialogue, which introduces the Eucharistic Prayer. Vatican II restored the integrity of the entire Eucharistic Prayer as a single entity and viewed the entire prayer as consecratory. To highlight both the unity and importance of the whole Eucharistic Prayer, all three eucharistic acclamations (the Sanctus, memorial acclamation, and great Amen) should normally be sung. It is equally appropriate that on feast days and some Sundays, presiders capable of singing might chant the entire Eucharistic Prayer to heighten its importance and solemnity. For this reason, musical tones are offered for each Eucharistic Prayer in the back of the Sacramentary.

A word is in order on a few technical items. The preface dialogue should not commence until the one presiding has found the proper page in the book for the preface to be used. This is infinitely better than for the presider to address the congregation with the words "Lift up your hearts!" and simultaneously flip through the Sacramentary searching for the right page. That communicates a very different message. Eye contact is a second important aspect of presiding at the Eucharist, especially during the Eucharistic Prayer. It is particularly appropriate that the presider look into the eyes of the assembly when they are addressed. They are, after all, the body of Christ. So the greeting "The Lord be with you" in the preface dialogue should be accompanied by eye contact that embraces those whom God has called together.

As the prayer continues, however, a certain balance is needed, since the presider should, first and foremost, be praying, not performing in the theatrical sense. Thus, to say, "Lord, you are holy indeed . . . ," while looking all around the church trying to make eye contact with members of the congregation does not give the impression that the presider is, in fact, praying (although he may well be doing so). Body language and bodily gestures are also critical, because they communicate wordlessly. Each presider needs to develop a particular style according to what feels most natural (e.g., how he extends his arms and the like). What is important, however, is to avoid gestures that appear artificial, stiff, or defensive. I knew a priest who would scream out, "Lift up your hearts!" at the assembly, with facial expressions that suggested he was almost spoiling for a fight!

The Sacramentary offers a variety of Eucharistic Prayers, some of which are especially appropriate for certain feasts and seasons. The presider will therefore need to give thought to this beforehand and become familiar enough with the text to pray it with grace and ease. Many opt for Eucharistic Prayer 2 because it is the shortest and most familiar, but to decide on that text for those reasons is to shortchange the assembly. Once a Eucharistic Prayer is chosen, however, improvising on the text is not recommended. I was once present at a Mass when the presider improvised on Eucharistic Prayer 3 in a way that completely changed the meaning of the text. He prayed: " . . . so that from east to west, from north to south, a perfect offering may be made. . . ." He apparently thought that the reference was geographical (e.g., from Montreal to Miami), when in fact it refers to the rising and setting of the sun. Improvising on the Eucharistic Prayer and other liturgical texts calls unnecessary attention to the presider and, ultimately, is a distraction.

Toward a Spirituality of Presiding

What can we say of a spirituality of presiding at the Liturgy of the Eucharist? I would suggest three key ingredients: prayerfulness, intentionality, and transparency.

First and most important, presiders need to be prayerful. This begins in contemplation long before they reach the sacristy to prepare for the liturgy, and it continues as they stand at the altar with arms outstretched. In other words, if those who stand at the table proclaiming the Eucharistic Prayer do not have a daily rhythm of personal prayer or meditation during the week, such prayerfulness will not magically happen when they stand before the assembly on Sunday morning.

Second, presiders need to be intentional about what they are doing. This means careful and reverent gestures that are not rushed or distracting. Whether bowing, incensing the altar, inviting the assembly into the Eucharistic Prayer with the words "Lift up your hearts!" or distributing Communion to those who come before them, presiders need to be fully engaged in the process.

Third, when presiders are prayerful and intentional, they will preside with transparency.

In short, presiding at the Liturgy of the Eucharist is not about the presider. It is about the service of God's reign that we celebrate and remember with holy food and drink. So the more a presider can stay out of the way and not draw attention to himself, the better. In the end, effective presiding at the Liturgy of the Eucharist should draw the whole community into that vision of the mystery of God that is both present among us and not yet fully revealed.

The Ministry of the Deacon

❀ ❀

Joseph DeGrocco

The Reverend Joseph DeGrocco is director of liturgical formation at the Seminary of the Immaculate Conception in Huntington, New York, and teaches homiletics in the permanent diaconate program in the Diocese of Rockville Centre, New York.

*A*lmost thirty-seven years have passed since Pope Paul VI set in motion the restoration of the permanent diaconate with his apostolic letter of June 18, 1967, Sacram Diaconatus Ordinem. One year after the promulgation of that letter, the bishops of the United States began restoring the permanent diaconate in this country. But even with all that has transpired in the intervening years, there is still much misinformation and confusion concerning this ordained ministry, even about its role in the liturgy.

Most Catholics are familiar with hearing about what sounds like two different diaconates. There are the "transitional deacons," who are ordained deacons as an interim step toward priesthood; and there are "permanent" deacons, those we often see ministering in parishes. Permanent deacons are usually married men well known in the community, husbands and fathers active in parish life, who have been ordained. Unfortunately, however—because the permanent diaconate had fallen out of sight for so many centuries, and the only deacons Catholics knew were men who were transitional deacons—when permanent deacons re-emerged on the scene, they were often thought of as "mini-priests." As a result, both laypeople and even some deacons themselves did not, and sometimes still do not, understand the permanent diaconate.

In all fairness, much of this confusion is understandable. We are still in the process of renewing our understanding of the sacrament of holy orders in general. By returning the church to its roots, the Second Vatican Council gave the church a renewed understanding of church life in many different areas. Perhaps this sense of recovering an ancient understanding of ministry is the best way to approach a clarification of the meaning of the diaconate in the church's liturgical life.

After Vatican II

What Vatican II initiated in this case can best be understood as the restoration of the order of deacons with its own identity. In other words, it must be seen as a full, permanent, and stable order in its own right. There is only one order of deacons, as the praenotanda to the Rite of Ordination of Deacons make clear: "Since there is but one diaconate, it is fitting that even in the celebration of ordination no distinction be made on the basis of the status of the candidates" (No. 183). As one of the ranks within the threefold ministry of holy orders—episcopacy, presbyterate, and diaconate—deacons have a distinct sacramental identity that is tied to the sacramental identity of the church itself. Vatican II recovered the ancient notion of the church as servant to the world, the Body of Christ that ministers to the world in order to help bring about its sanctification and redemption. This is the sacramental identity of the deacon, ordained to *diakonia,* or service.

This mission of charity and service oriented toward the salvation of all people is highlighted in the ordination rite and is essential to understanding the restoration of the order of deacons.

Unfortunately, many Catholics look upon a permanent deacon as simply a man who has been given permission (or even more unfortunately, the "power") to dress in vestments and function liturgically, and then, incidentally, to do other things as well in the name of the church. Truly impoverished is the deacon who understands his ministry primarily as a liturgical one.

Historically, a deacon was admitted to service at the eucharistic table because he served at the table of the poor. It was his service in and to the world that provided the context for his liturgical service. This is why, for example, the deacon is the one to announce petitions of the prayers of the faithful (the General Intercessions). As one who worked directly with the sick, the poor, and the needy in the community, the deacon intimately knew their needs and brought those needs to the attention of the praying community as a whole.

This also helps us understand the liturgical functioning of the deacon in general. The General Instruction of the Roman Missal sees the deacon as holding "first place among those who minister in the eucharistic celebration" (No. 94). Although a deacon cannot preside at the Eucharist (that is, he cannot "celebrate Mass"), the Roman rite envisions the deacon's actions as a normative part of the Eucharist, along with the ministries of reader, server, and cantor. Thus the various roles that make up the Body of Christ, not just the role of the priest-presider, show Christ's presence more fully.

In one sense, the liturgical functioning of the deacon might be seen as a kind of "mediator" between the priest and the people. The functioning of a deacon as an ordained minister at Mass helps us to avoid a misguided overemphasis on the power of the priesthood—as if the role of the priest, though essential and irreplaceable, were the only important role at Mass. The deacon authentically sacramentalizes this role at the liturgy to the degree that he is intimately involved with those who are most in need of the church's ministry: the poor, the sick, and the needy. He is the link that helps the assembly "lift up their hearts" to the Lord in the eucharistic sacrifice. The suggested homily for the rite of ordination makes clear this connection between diaconal service and liturgical offering: "Holding the mystery of faith with a clear conscience, express by your actions the word of God which your lips proclaim, so that the Christian people, brought to life by the Spirit, may be a pure offering accepted by God" (No. 199).

It is exactly this presence in the world that gives the diaconate its unique sacramental identity. The deacon is one who is called to bring the ministry of the church—its mission of charity and justice— to the workplace, to the community, to the neighborhood, and to all the places in which he lives and interacts with others daily.

The Deacon at Mass

The General Instruction is clear concerning the liturgical functioning of the deacon at Mass. Remember that the document sees the unity and life of the church as manifested in the participation of the members according to their different orders and offices. Remember also, as mentioned earlier, that the deacon holds "first place among those who minister in the eucharistic celebration" (No. 94). Thus, there is a distinction between the presidential functions belonging to the priest-celebrant alone and the ministerial functions belonging to others, and the deacon is seen as the first among those who function in a ministerial way at Mass. The functions specifically assigned to the deacon are: proclaiming the Gospel; sometimes preaching God's word; announcing the intentions of the Prayers of the Faithful; preparing the altar; serving the celebration of the Sacrifice; distributing the Eucharist to the faithful, especially the Precious Blood; and sometimes giving directions to the people for their proper gestures and posture.

Let's take a closer look at some of these functions.

From the beginning of Mass, the deacon's special relationship with the proclamation of the Gospel is made evident: it is the deacon who carries the Book of Gospels, slightly elevated, in the entrance procession. In some sense, the Book of Gospels might be seen as the deacon's book since the deacon is entrusted with proclaiming the Gospel at Mass. Obviously, the liturgical proclamation of the Gospel is of the utmost importance, and deacons must be good proclaimers. All the basic skills of good public speaking, along with a spirituality and education rooted in the Gospels, must be a part of this liturgical function.

Although it may be done by the priest or by some other minister, it is customary for the deacon to announce the invocations of the Penitential Rite at the beginning of Mass when Form C is used (i.e., three invocations: the responses being "Lord have mercy / Christ have mercy / Lord have mercy" in succession). These invocations are addressed to Christ, and should focus on Christ's redemptive work, not on our own unworthiness. The invocations express who Christ is or what Christ has done/is doing. They are not acts of penance by which we make ourselves worthy to celebrate the Eucharist. As a result, the forms in the Sacramentary, or other forms modeled on those, should be the only ones used; expressions such as, "For the times that we . . ." are not appropriate.

After reading the Gospel, the deacon normally announces the intentions of the Prayers of the Faithful (the General Intercessions). These prayers directly connect the deacon's liturgical ministry with his ministry to the poor, sick, and needy in the workplace and community, as described above. It is therefore crucial that the deacon know how to announce these intentions so that they are invitations to moments of prayer for the assembly. Understanding the various clauses that are often a part of the petitions and making appropriate pauses (especially after the intention is announced, but before saying, "Let us pray to the Lord") are aids to announcing these intentions well. He also must be absolutely certain to pronounce names correctly when they are to be read as part of the prayers for the sick, the dying, and the deceased. Ideally, the deacon is familiar with the names because he is familiar with the sick and the dying persons from his ministering to them.

Next the deacon assists at the altar. He prepares the altar with the corporal and the missal, takes care of the sacred vessels, assists the priest in receiving the gifts, and prepares the chalice. When necessary, he may assist the priest with the chalice or the missal throughout the Liturgy of the Eucharist. Yet it is clear that the deacon does not in any way concelebrate. For example, during the Eucharistic Prayer, while the deacon stands near the priest, he does so slightly behind him. (Anecdotally, this is important not only for reasons of liturgical theology, but also for practicality. As a presider, I like to extend my arms in a very wide *orans* position, and assisting deacons sometimes find themselves coming in "contact" with my open hand, so to speak, if they stand too close or crowd the altar!) Also during the Eucharistic Prayer, from the *epiclesis* until the priest shows the chalice, the deacon normally kneels. At the doxology that concludes the Eucharistic Prayer, the deacon, standing next to the priest, elevates the chalice while the priest elevates the paten with the host.

In receiving Holy Communion, the deacon does not self-communicate; he receives Communion under both kinds from the priest, and then assists in distributing Holy Communion. The General Instruction consistently notes that the deacon administers the chalice to the people. He then assists after Communion in consuming whatever remains of the Eucharist and in bringing the sacred vessels to the credence table. As a minister at the altar, the deacon should see to the clearing of the altar after Communion, just as he was responsible for its preparation before the presentation of the gifts.

Finally, it is the deacon's role to direct the assembly and to give directions to the assembly as needed. He proclaims, "Let us offer each other the sign of peace," invites the people to bow their heads for God's blessing if a solemn blessing is used by the priest, and dismisses the assembly at the end of the Mass after the final blessing. At other times he might have to announce brief directions concerning the assembly's gestures or posture. Whenever he does so, these directions should be simple and to the point; they should not be overly casual nor disruptive to the unity and flow of the entire ritual.

Everything that the deacon does as one of the ministers at Mass should enhance the prayer and active participation of the entire assembly, and facilitate the smooth functioning of the other ministers. The deacon must not "co-preside" at Mass, nor should he draw attention to himself in any way. Rather, as the first among ministers, he is there to serve the active participation of the faithful and to assist the priest as the presider. Consequently, the deacon at Mass should be transparent so that it is clearly Christ who shines through as he is present in his Body that gathers for worship, a liturgical presence made manifest in the variety of liturgical roles.

The Good Deacon

What are the qualities of a good deacon? While the following list is not exhaustive and not in any particular order of importance, I think these aspects represent a bare minimum.

- *An understanding of being called by God and a desire to pursue holiness.* A man pursuing the diaconate must

see his desire to serve as a true vocation. Essential to
that calling is a commitment to the person and mission
of Jesus Christ, a commitment that includes a willingness and ability to live such Gospel values as simplicity
of life, compassion and forgiveness, humility, and obedience. Inherent in this call to holiness is the mature
understanding of his own identity as a disciple and
as a deacon. As such, it is obvious that the permanent
diaconate is not something just for retired men. It is
a calling to service and to ministry that is appropriate for a man of any age. Nor is the permanent diaconate just something that represents a "next step" for a
man who has long been involved in parish life and is
looking for the next thing to do. Rather, it is a gift to
the church that has its own charism and brings its own
contribution to the life of the church.

- *A willingness to be a man of the church.* Deacons have
  a special relationship to the bishop. Their service to
  the church is through their relationship to the bishop
  and their obedience to him, promised at ordination.
  Since most permanent deacons serve in their home
  parish, some Catholics assume that they are ordained
  for their parish and are linked to their pastor, but this
  is not true. For example, in my own diocese, Rockville
  Centre, New York, it is commonly understood that
  permanent deacons will not serve in their home parish
  automatically. Instead, they are assigned by the bishop
  according to the needs of the diocese, in order to allow
  them to function where they are most needed. Such
  an equitable distribution of deacons throughout the
  diocese is especially important with the ever-growing

priest shortage and is also a more accurate reflection of our common life as a diocesan church.

This aspect of the diaconal vocation was described very powerfully to me by Thomas Bast, a deacon in our diocese who requested that our bishop transfer his assignment from his home parish—where he and his wife had resided for twenty-five years and where their children received most of their sacraments—to a parish that had just been "downsized" to a one-priest parish. Deacon Tom described it thus: "My calling to the diaconate always involved an understanding on my part that the primary reason for becoming a deacon was to be of service where needed. It meant walking away from everything that was good and comfortable, but I kept coming back to my primary reason for answering the call to become a deacon: to serve where needed. All of this meant a greater sacrifice on my part. But isn't that what *diakonia* is all about: to put the needs of others ahead of our own needs and wants?"

- *A willingness to be intimately involved with the needs of the sick, the poor, and the needy.* Given their call to sacramentalize the church's mission of service, deacons must be in the midst of the community, serving the needs of the poor, the forgotten, and the neglected. The traditional scriptural foundation for the church's *diakonia* is found in chapter 6 of the Acts of the Apostles, in which seven men of good repute are prayed over and have hands laid on them in order to minister to the Greek-speaking widows neglected in the daily distribution of food. Service at the table of the poor precedes, and in a sense is a prerequisite for, service at the altar. Without such service, the diaconate becomes an empty clerical rank within the church hierarchy.

In our diocese, men preparing for the diaconate are increasingly aware of this important aspect of their formation. Four deacon candidates traveled recently with two ordained deacons to our diocesan mission in the Dominican Republic. Thomas Reilly, one of the candidates, explained how the trip transformed his view of mission work from one of just a functional "giving money to poor people" to a real solidarity with them: "It was amazing how the people of the Dominican Republic illustrated that the people are the church," he told me. "We have heard it stated before; many of us believe it to be true. But we had never experienced the spirit of church working through the followers of Jesus as clearly as on this trip. We learned that the table of the Lord can be a stool placed on a dirt floor, and that Jesus can be fully worshiped there. You can see what love, devotion, community, and celebration are all about."

- *The ability to be a "man of community," calling forth the gifts of all the baptized.* As one who has a foot in both the world of the laity and that of the clergy, the deacon is in a unique position to build up the body of Christ, and to promote the gifts and ministries of all the baptized. The deacon must be especially aware of both the individualism and anti-institutional bias rampant today: He must be one who gives witness to the necessity of Communion and our responsibility to one another in the Body of Christ.

- *The personal integrity to balance family, work, and service to the church.* As an ordained minister, the deacon has the responsibility to give public witness in the name of the church by following Christ in all areas of his life—his marriage, his family, his secular occupation, and his style of life. This is a daunting task. The homily in the rite of ordination says it well: "Like those once chosen by the apostles for the ministry of charity, you should be men of good reputation, filled with wisdom and the Holy Spirit. Firmly rooted and grounded in faith, you are to show yourselves chaste and beyond reproach before God and man, as is proper for the ministers of Christ and the stewards of God's mysteries" (No. 199).

- *The ability to be a man of the word.* Although his ministry is supposed to be much broader than just the liturgical ministry of functioning at Mass, the fact is that most people come into contact with deacons in precisely this role, as ministers of the word at Mass. It is the deacon who is charged with proclaiming the Gospel during the celebration of the Eucharist. But as with his service at the table of the altar, this ministry at the table of the word should stem from his being a man of the word in every aspect of his life. In the ordination rite, the ordaining bishop places the book of the Gospels in the hands of the newly ordained deacon and says, "Receive the Gospel of Christ, whose herald you have become. Believe what you read, teach what you believe, and practice what you teach." A deacon is also empowered to preach at Mass. Thus, as a minister of God's word, the deacon must allow the power of Scripture to pervade every aspect of his life. He must constantly be meditating on the word and applying it to his life, so that by both preaching and example he

shows how the word of God can be active in the hearts
and minds of all who follow Christ.

Ministry to the World

Seeing the order of deacons as a separate and distinct order lies at
the heart of understanding this ordained ministry. There should
be no desire, then, to ordain permanent deacons as priests as an
answer to the priest shortage, since this would make the diaconate nothing more than a stepping-stone or a mini-priesthood.
The church is best served when all three levels of holy orders—
bishop, priest, and deacon—are fully evident in the community.
Jesus Christ is most fully sacramentalized in the church's ministry to the world only when the order of *diakonia* is fully understood, recognized, and appreciated as a stable, permanent order
of its own.

The Ministry
of the Lector

James M. Schellman

James M. Schellman is executive director of The North American Forum on the Catechumenate, a network of parish and diocesan ministers dedicated to the implementation of the Rite of Christian Initiation of Adults.

R oman Catholics have not generally been thought of as people of the word, that is, of the Bible. This has been considered one of the dividing lines between Catholics and other Christians for nearly five hundred years.

The past thirty-some years, however, have witnessed a sea of change in biblical familiarity among Catholics. This is mostly a result of the Scripture now enshrined in our own language throughout Catholic worship. For most of us, this word is experienced especially through the biblical readings proclaimed, preached, and savored Sunday after Sunday during the Liturgy of the Word at Mass.

Contrast our present Sunday experience with the way it used to be. Formerly, the priest read the Scriptures—first in Latin at the altar with his back to the people, and then in English at the pulpit. The readings were passages from the epistles and Gospels arranged in one set of Scripture readings that was repeated year after year. On Sundays a homily usually followed, but rarely did the homily have much to do with the Scripture passages just heard.

The present Lectionary for Mass must be viewed as one of the most remarkably effective achievements of the church in centuries. Through it the Catholic community as a whole now experiences the biblical word in corporate worship in a breadth and depth unknown for hundreds of years. Over the course of a three-year cycle of readings and psalms, we now have proclaimed and preached most of the New Testament and carefully chosen selections from the Old Testament, including the poetic words of the psalms. This prayerful communal discipline is forming us in ways we can only begin to imagine.

This worship experience has proved so winning that many of our Christian sisters and brothers in North America and other parts of the world now use an ecumenical version of this Lectionary (called the Common Lectionary) for their Sunday worship. Among these communities are the Lutherans, United Methodists, Anglicans, Presbyterians, and the United Church. It is wonderful that after centuries of division, we are, in fact, in union at the table of the word with these fellow believers. Who would have thought this possible even a few years ago? But the full flowering of this Spirit-inspired development is still before us.

A Sacramental Presence

The power and significance of the biblical word at worship can be glimpsed in the early experience of the church. During times of persecution, lectors—readers whose ministry was to prepare and proclaim the word at worship—were among those local church leaders who were particular targets. The proclamation of Scripture was perceived by the persecuting authorities for what it was: a powerful and galvanizing force for Christian presence and action in the world.

A renewed understanding of the importance and power of this liturgical ministry led to its restoration in our time. Providentially, this restored ministry has as its purpose to break open the far richer treasury of biblical readings now available to the Catholic people at worship. This is symbolized by the bound Lectionary itself. Over the centuries it had become part of the book of Mass prayers used by the priest-celebrant. (This development coincided with the gradual absorption of various roles in the liturgy by the ordained.) The ministry of the reader once again has its own liturgical book, as does the ministry of the priest-celebrant.

The deep significance of this ministry lies in its close connection with the contemporary recovery of a fuller sacramental understanding of our Catholic worship. All of us need to become more deeply immersed in the church's ongoing renewal of understanding of the word in that worship. Consider, for example, this observation from the Second Vatican Council's "Constitution on Divine Revelation" (Dei Verbum):

> The church has always venerated the divine Scriptures just as she venerates the body of the Lord, since from the table of both the word of God and of the body of Christ she unceasingly receives and offers to the faithful the bread of life, especially in the sacred liturgy. (No. 21)

In other words, there are two tables at Mass, the table of the word and the table of the Lord's body and blood. Together they constitute a single place of worship before God. And it is from each of these tables that we are fed, that we receive the bread of life. Implicit in this teaching is the understanding of the real presence of Christ now embraced by the church:

> For at the celebration of Mass, which perpetuates the sacrifice of the cross, Christ is really present in the assembly gathered in his name; he is present in the person of the minister, in his own word, and indeed substantially and permanently under the eucharistic elements. (General Instruction of the Roman Missal, chapter 2, No. 7)

It remained for the Introduction to the Lectionary for Mass to bring out the intimate and indivisible link between the Lord's presence in these two tables; that is, at the Liturgy of the Word and the Liturgy of the Eucharist:

> As a help toward celebrating the memorial of the Lord with eager devotion, the faithful should be keenly aware of the one presence of Christ in both the word of God—it is he himself "who speaks when the sacred Scriptures are read in the church"—and "above all under the eucharistic species." (No. 46)

The Word as Communion

In this light, we can discern in the Liturgy of the Word and the Liturgy of the Eucharist something resembling the parallel rituals of proclamation and Communion. In both liturgies we show reverence for the presence of the Lord. These are perhaps more obvious to us in the Liturgy of the Eucharist, with bows, genuflections, kneeling, the showing of the eucharistic elements at the consecration, the deliberate and reverent extension of hands for the eucharistic bread and cup, and the many other signs of reverence that individuals choose to make.

Consider the similar signs of reverence during the Liturgy of the Word: the solemn announcement of each reading; the reverent listening to the proclamation of the readings; the special responses after the readings, especially the one following the proclamation of the Gospel that acknowledges the Lord's presence; and the other signs associated with the Gospel readings—the posture of standing, the Gospel procession with use of candles and incense, the sign of the cross made on the book and by members of the assembly, and the final kissing of the book.

Consider next the similar ritual flow of the rituals of word and table. The Liturgy of the Eucharist achieves its "center and high point" in the Eucharistic Prayer, the solemn proclamation of God's saving deeds. In this proclamation bread and wine become the Lord's body and blood. In the strength of this presence, the assembly offers prayers of intercession for the church, the world, and the deceased, and prays for the unity of the church. This solemn proclamation brings us to the breaking of the eucharistic bread and the pouring of the eucharistic wine, actions consummated in eucharistic Communion. In receiving the Lord's body and blood, we are made one with him and one another as food and drink for a world beloved of and longing for God in Christ.

In the Liturgy of the Word, the readings culminate in the solemn proclamation of the Gospel. This leads to the homily, a breaking open of the proclaimed word for the nourishment of the assembly. This Communion in the Lord, present in the word, is then extended during a period of communal silence, a time for savoring that word in the hearts of the assembly. Strengthened by this nourishment, the assembly then brings to the table its priestly prayers of intercession for the church, the world, and those in particular need.

Proclaiming the Word

In this light, it becomes apparent that the ministry of the reader at Mass is pivotal to the whole liturgical celebration. At stake is the experience of the sacramental presence of the Lord, both in the word and Communion and with one another.

Effective proclamation of the word, therefore, is an intrinsic part of the whole celebration. Spoken communication is first of all a human reality, requiring the use of simple human skills. As was declared over four hundred years ago at the Council of Trent, "sacraments are for people"; that is, bodily spirits destined for resurrected life.

To proclaim the biblical word at worship with little or no interpretive emphasis is just as misguided as to proclaim it with too much. Last year on the Third Sunday of Advent, I heard one reader render the magnificent passage from St. Paul's Letter to the Philippians in an utterly deadpan way. I was appalled at the travesty of hearing, "Rejoice in the Lord always. I shall say it again: rejoice!," delivered dully. Interpretation is not a choice; it is inevitable. It begins the moment the reader steps to the ambo. The challenge is to bring to the reading the telling combination of prayerful, intelligent preparation as well as the unique personality and skill that each reader possesses.

Above all, the readers must understand and believe that they are performing a real ministry of presence and communion. They must accept that the Lord is active and present to the assembly through their proclamation, that the Lord longs to speak and be heard in the biblical word they enunciate. It is a word for this assembly, here and now, and each of its members is called to hear and respond to that word today, this week, over the coming weeks.

By the words with which the reading concludes, "The Word of the Lord," the reader invites the assembly to acknowledge the Lord's presence, as does the eucharistic minister with the words "The Body of Christ." I recall the first time I experienced a reader make a real pause at the end of a reading, and then, looking full at the assembly, announce "The Word of the Lord" with a gentle deliberation that made one feel invited to receive that word with joyful assent: "Thanks be to God!"

Further, as the church has long taught, in Communion we become what we receive. In receiving and celebrating God's word alive in our midst, we become the Lord's own presence and long for a world better than the one we have helped shape. We become in Christ that transforming word to the world, the means by which it is transformed into what God intended from all time.

The Unique Word

Lectors need to understand all this and more. When I have the privilege of forming readers for this ministry, I do not begin with the elements of public proclamation. Skills development is the last step. Instead, I invite them first of all to a deep and honest reflection on their own journey in and with Christ. As the Scriptures tell us, this is the Christ who became "sin itself" for our salvation. In other words, God in Christ has entered into the very brokenness of the great story that began in that first garden and continues to unfold uniquely in each one of us. We need to bring all that we are into God's presence. It is our full human experience that God addresses in the Scriptures. Nothing must be left out. And all must be transformed.

So I try to help these ministers of the word learn how that word ministers first of all to them. But before turning to training in the skills of public proclamation, another critical formative step must occur. I invite them to imagine the personal stories of those to whom they proclaim this living word. They only need to recall their own journey in Christ—its ups and downs, its heartbreak, failures, and unutterable longings—in order to communicate this to those who look up expectantly at the announcement that this is "A reading from . . ."

Hundreds of similar stories abound in the hearts and minds of those who struggle to hear the Lord in this word: children, parents, single people, straight, gay, lifelong Catholics, catechumens coming to Mass fresh and expectant, those who have lost those they love, those who have failed those who love them. To each and all, the Lord now speaks a unique word, and the reader is God's chosen instrument in that very moment of its communication: "The Word of the Lord!"

The Ministry
❀ of the Parish Liturgy ❀
Committee

Kathy A. Lindell

*Kathy A. Lindell is the former director of the Office for Worship of the
Archdiocese of Los Angeles. Before this position, she served for fifteen
years in the Office for Worship and also, for twenty years, as a member
of her parish liturgy committee.*

*I*f we think of Sunday Mass as a sacred drama with two or
three acts, several scenes, numerous props, and a cast composed of presider, deacon, assembly, servers, lectors, eucharistic ministers, hospitality ministers, and a choir, it is easy to see
the reason for the rise and spread of parish liturgy committees
since the Second Vatican Council. Someone has to plan and put
all this together in accordance with the church's norms and the
people's needs. But the church's worship is not just a set of texts
and rubrics. Liturgy committees exist principally to enhance the
living experience of the people of God as they come together in
yearning to sustain the vision of a kingdom come in Jesus Christ.

The Revised General Instruction of the Roman Missal notes
the importance of "directions about the preparation of people's
hearts and minds, and of the places, rites, and texts for the celebration of the Most Holy Eucharist" (No. 1). It clearly acknowledges that since liturgy is the "primary and indispensable source
from which the faithful are to derive the true Christian Spirit . . .
the entire celebration is planned in such a way that it leads to a

conscious, active, and full participation of the faithful both in body and mind" (No. 18).

Although there is no scriptural basis for the team that prepares the liturgy, we have the example of Saints Peter and John preparing the Passover meal for Jesus and his disciples. We can also assume from other scriptural references, as well as early church documents, that when the church gathered each Sunday to celebrate, someone saw to it that people were welcomed, the site appropriately arranged, and the prayers, stories, and the Scriptures prepared. Egeria, a Spanish pilgrim who was present at the liturgies in Jerusalem during one Holy Week in the fourth century, expressed admiration in her writings for one of the traits of the Jerusalem liturgy: the selection of scriptural texts had been adapted to the circumstances of the time.

From the earliest years of implementation of the liturgical reform envisioned by the Second Vatican Council, Catholics have responded with generosity to the call to serve as liturgy committee members. Principles and practices that lead to effective liturgy committees have emerged over the years, as have many challenges. All of them illustrate the complex realities of parish life, and the gifts and tensions of people as they deal with diverse experiences and ecclesiologies.

Good Practices

What, then, can bring everyone together? What can empower liturgy committees to soar beyond their very human, and therefore limited, vision into the mystery and Spirit-filled imagination of God? The liturgy itself invites us into this imagination by showing us how we might know more deeply what it means to live, die, and rise with Christ. The ministry of the liturgy committee is to live out the paschal mystery.

What are good practices for liturgy committees that can lead to full celebration of this mystery? And what are some of the challenges?

- Parish leaders should understand that, because liturgy is at the heart of all parish life, the liturgy committee and its work need to be among the highest priorities. The committee's needs and recommendations should be reflected in the parish mission statement, the allocation of financial resources and staffing, and the prominence given liturgy in religious education programs. The mission statement of one Midwestern parish, for example, inspires a powerful mandate for ministry by clearly affirming Christ as the center and liturgy as the source and summit of the Christian life: "We are the body of Christ at St. Nicholas Parish, Evanston, Illinois, called to gather for worship, cherish the traditions of our faith, witness the Gospel, minister to others, be Christians in the world." But practical matters like salaries also require close attention. A parish in southern California discovered that a gifted music director was considering resigning because he was not being paid what he considered a living wage. The committee reviewed his salary with the finance committee, which not only adjusted his pay, but also initiated a review of all the salaries in the parish.

- The parish liturgy committee should understand that its primary responsibility is not to prepare liturgical ceremonies. Rather, the committee should focus on the full range of the parish's liturgical life. This includes budgeting, long- and short-range planning, establishing parish liturgy policy, developing job descriptions for liturgical ministers, evaluating liturgies, and continuing the formation and education in liturgy for committee members and the assembly. Other questions should be considered: Who actually prepares the liturgy? Who works to shape the ritual and the environment, selects the music, considers possibilities for the homily, and orchestrates the many other particulars of the liturgy?

- Liturgy is a work of art, and therefore, should be prepared by artists. These artists should be drawn as much as possible from the congregation itself, as should other parishioners they are forming and training. Parish leaders need to work diligently to identify liturgical artists, whose training and education in music, ritual movement, poetry, and environmental art are focused on the liturgy, past and present, and its central role in the life of the church. Committees with assemblies of diverse backgrounds have a great responsibility because their "artists" must discern how to express and celebrate unity in the midst of great diversity.

  Parishes that want to be successful in meeting these goals should try to form committees that exchange views respectfully and frequently (sometimes in more than one language). These dialogues should focus on a cultural understanding and experience of liturgy, music, dance, and visual arts, as well as on family prayer and meal-sharing customs. One such dialogue was begun in California by a parish music director with a doctorate in ethnomusicology. She invited the Hispanic people in her music groups, whose experience was as diverse as their countries of origin, to share their knowledge and experience of All Souls Day—also known in Hispanic areas as the Day of the Dead. Their discussions transformed the parish's celebration of All Souls Day by leading to the adoption of new and more culturally friendly modes of liturgical expression. Word of their process spread and inspired dialogue in other parishes among Asians, African Americans, and other cultural groups, who also honor their ancestors and the dead with their own traditional prayers and rituals.

- Effective leadership is vital. Committee members should have integrity, flexibility, courage, humility, and a passion for making things better because they understand the power of the liturgy to transform hearts, lives, and communities. Their leadership skills should be supported by the group leader, and by prayer and surrender of self to God. In practical ways this means that liturgy committee members must be willing and able to explain and defend the decisions of the committee to the parish-at-large. They need to muster the courage to challenge respectfully the parish staff and others in authority. They should fight with passion and conviction for what they believe in but should also be willing to support decisions based on alternative points of view.

- Committee members should be willing to hold one another accountable, and have the courage to face difficult issues with honesty. If the music and choir directors, for example, regularly select music that the assembly cannot sing, the committee should propose more appropriate songs. If parish resources are spread too thinly over six Masses each Sunday and the church is less than half-full at some of these, the committee should consider eliminating one or more of the Masses and adjusting the Mass schedule. If liturgy committee meetings are poorly planned and mismanaged, the members need to speak up and be willing to hold accountable those who are responsible, including themselves.

• The committee and the pastor need to be clear about who makes the final decisions. In some parishes, the pastor decides; in others, a small, designated team, usually paid staff, has the final say. Decision by consensus is another option. When I served as director of the Office for Worship in Los Angeles, both pastors and committee members frequently expressed confusion and frustration about decision making. Usually my response was simple: "Put the issue out front. Then keep talking and listening to one another until the issue is clearly understood by everyone who has decision-making power. Then hold one another accountable for what everyone understands."

Other situations call for a process to help build relationships and trust. One parish worker told me, "Our new pastor will hardly let us do anything!" I asked her what he *would* let them do and suggested that for the time being they work hard at doing that task exceedingly well. One year later, the same person called and told me that the pastor was gradually expanding the committee's decision-making responsibilities because he was learning to trust them. The committee's respect for him was also growing.

• Liturgy committee members should honor, respect, and continue to grow in their understanding of theological, historical, spiritual, pastoral, and juridical principles of liturgy. Liturgical competence, especially on the part of the presider, is essential. The Second Vatican Council's Sacrosanctum Concilium states that priests especially must be "imbued with the spirit and power of the liturgy." My experience at our diocesan worship office taught me that many priests strive tirelessly and with deep commitment to achieve this goal, but some do not. The General Instruction affirms the importance of the ministry and leadership of the priest-celebrant. I have observed countless priests welcoming and embracing this call to liturgical leadership. They worked with one another, their liturgy committees, and others to be formed in their role as the one who presides. Others, unfortunately, acted out of clericalism, ignorance, or indifference, making unilateral decisions because of a too-strict adherence to rubrics, personal biases, and preferences, or in response to pressure from a vocal few in the parish.

This can be especially difficult when a new pastor comes into a parish that has a strong and established tradition of vibrant, faith-filled liturgies, and almost immediately begins to impose his personal agenda. New pastors would do well to worship with the assembly and participate in its liturgical practices for at least a year before suggesting any changes. Liturgy committees that have worked effectively in a spirit of collegiality will dissolve if a new pastor arbitrarily ignores their dedication, hard work, expertise, and experience. By the same token, pastors who experience hostility or disrespect for their role as presider may avoid meetings or even consider disbanding the committee.

- The liturgy committee must know, love, and respect the assembly. Establishing this kind of relationship and understanding is as basic to the committee's success as knowing the ages, ethnicities, cultures, socioeconomic statuses, and education levels of the parishioners. It is vital if the committee hopes to be in touch with the assembly, or to understand and support the way it prays, sings, and listens liturgically.

Parishes all over the country are discovering that learning about the people who assemble each Sunday is not a matter of demographic fact-finding or reading the latest book on multicultural liturgy (although these can help). It requires experiences that deepen the relationships that can profoundly influence liturgical prayer. These may include meal-sharing, with various ethnic and cultural foods on the table; seminars and retreats that encourage dialogue and sharing of stories and values; and intergenerational and multicultural social gatherings, with music and dancing.

- A liturgical committee should center its primary attention on doing the basics exceptionally well, Sunday after Sunday—the fundamental actions of gathering, welcoming, proclaiming the Word, and celebrating the Eucharist. The committee members must identify clearly what needs to be done and pursue solutions honestly, with respect for the demands of the liturgy. If the Liturgy of the Word needs improving, for example, the committee should be willing to consider a broad range of areas to work on. Among these might be the quality of proclamation and the homily; ritual movement; the sound system; the appearance of the Lectionary and Book of Gospels; catechesis for the assembly about liturgical silence, listening, and response; religious education and Scripture study that are Lectionary–based; and weekly reflection on the Scriptures with homilists. But liturgy committees also need to be realistic about what they can accomplish with often limited time and resources.

- Members of the committee should believe that evaluation matters. The evaluation should consist of concrete observations offered by people with a vision that goes beyond Sunday. Comments should clearly indicate in detail what promotes "conscious, active, and full participation," and what hinders it. More important, the committee should know that participation is not just about what happens on Sunday. People's lives and the life of their community should be transformed by their worship and prayer. Participation in and support of parish soup kitchens and outreach, such as prison ministry and care for the homeless or shut-ins, are just a few examples of another kind of "liturgy," one that is experienced beyond just Sunday.

- Finally, liturgy committee members should enter fully into the liturgical life of the parish. They should freely and reverently open their hearts to the awesome experience of confronting the image of God in Christ gathered, proclaimed, blessed, broken, and shared. They must also grapple with what this confrontation calls them to be and to do in their own lives, as well as at liturgy committee meetings.

Good liturgy committee practices like those described in this essay develop over time. Each group of people can begin only as God begins with each of us—exactly where we are. A thoughtful and prayerful assessment of current practices and a commitment to move forward, one step at a time, are a good start. Liturgy committee members who accept God's call to enter fully into the celebration of Lent and its liturgies, with sincere and courageous hearts, open to conversion in their lives and ministry, will arrive at the great Easter Vigil—and the next liturgy committee meeting— renewed and more deeply formed in the joy of the Resurrection.

Through this joy, they will know what it means to prepare and celebrate Sunday as exemplified by the Opening Prayer for the Second Sunday of Easter: "We no longer look for Jesus among the dead, for he is alive and has become the Lord of life. From the waters of death you raise us with him and renew your gift of life within us. Increase in our minds and hearts the risen life we share with Christ and help us to grow as your people toward the fullness of eternal life with you."

❀ Music Ministry ❀

J. Michael McMahon

J. Michael McMahon is president of the National Association of Pastoral Musicians in Silver Spring, Maryland.

embers of the assembly always seem to pay greater attention to some elements of the liturgical celebration than to others. Conventional wisdom among parish leaders has long held that Sunday worshipers go home talking mainly about two aspects of the Sunday liturgy: the homily and the music.

The importance of music for parish liturgical celebrations points to the pastoral role of liturgical musicians. This pastoral aspect of music ministry is so significant that *pastoral* is included in the name of the largest organization of Catholic church musicians in the United States (some nine thousand strong): the National Association of Pastoral Musicians (N.A.P.M.).

Music directors occasionally receive letters from parishioners describing how the music of a particular celebration changed their lives. One year, after an exhausting Holy Week and Easter Triduum, I received a letter from a thirty-five-year-old mother of two. She had participated in the Easter Sunday morning Mass, at which the music ministers consisted of a forty-voice choir and

a cantor, accompanied by organ and brass. Most of the music, including familiar Easter hymns, was sung robustly by the whole assembly. The choir also sang alone, including a choral setting of the Easter Sequence and the "Hallelujah Chorus" from Handel's *Messiah*. After weeks of intense rehearsals and three days of singing for the major liturgies of the triduum, the choir was tired but exhilarated. The congregation sang the liturgy vigorously, and the choir led them with a joy that transcended physical weariness.

This woman had come to Mass on that Easter morning after a long absence from the church and was expecting very little. But she found herself enveloped in an assembly that participated energetically in singing the Mass and was inspired by the choir, organ, and brass, the combination of which communicated a profound sense of faith in the power of Christ's new life. Not only did this woman return to the practice of the faith, but she soon found her way into music ministry as a member of the parish choir.

Pastoral musicians can cite many such examples of the ways in which music helps people connect the celebration of the liturgy with their own lives of faith. These connections are most obvious on occasions such as baptisms or funerals, or during particular seasons and feasts, such as Christmas or Lent. Sometimes music speaks to people most clearly at times of personal crisis. I recall one Sunday when, during the Communion procession, my eyes met those of a woman who had suffered a miscarriage during the previous week. We were singing, "Unless a grain of wheat shall fall upon the ground and die, it remains just a grain of wheat with no life." After an interval of many years, both of us still recall that profound moment of recognition.

Musicians are perhaps less accustomed to receiving letters, calls, and comments of affirmation than those of complaint. People often ask: Why don't we sing hymns to the Blessed Virgin Mary during Sunday Masses in May? Why can't the music be more

traditional or more contemporary, more upbeat, more familiar, more varied? Why don't we have less (or more) music from other cultures, less (or more) Gregorian chant, less (or more) youth-oriented music, less (or more) music by the choir alone, less (or more) music with organ or contemporary ensemble or rock band? Sometimes musicians hear these questions not just from parishioners, but even from their bishops and pastors.

These questions point to several significant issues that liturgical musicians face as they work to serve the pastoral needs of their communities, as well as to provide competent musical leadership and to foster good liturgical celebration.

Participation and Performance

Prior to the Second Vatican Council, most choirs and organists thought of their role as "providing music" for the liturgy. Of course, official church documents since the publication in 1903 of Inter Sollicitudines, issued by Pope St. Pius X, had encouraged active singing of Latin chants and responses of the liturgy by the whole congregation. Still, before the Second Vatican Council most Catholics experienced a liturgy in which all the singing was performed by a choir or one singer (who often was also the organist).

The liturgical reforms of the Second Vatican Council represented both continuity and change in the way that music would be used. As in all official church documents since 1903, Sacrosanctum Concilium emphasized the singing of the liturgical texts: acclamations, responses, antiphons, psalms, and songs. The S.C. includes an entire chapter on sacred music, declaring its value to be, "[G]reater even than that of any other art. The main reason for this pre-eminence is that, as sacred song closely bound to the text, it forms a necessary or integral part of the solemn liturgy" (No. 112). The constitution also reiterated the dual purpose of music in the liturgy: the glorification of God and the sanctification of the faithful.

The Second Vatican Council set out a new agenda for liturgical musicians in its insistence on the active participation of the entire assembly in the singing of the liturgy. Sacrosanctum Concilium charged those responsible for the revision of the liturgical books to consider this active participation before any other element. The role of choirs and other musicians was reaffirmed, but they were now to carry out their ministry with due regard for the active role of the assembly.

While many choirs were downgraded or eliminated in the years immediately following the council, it soon became clear that the role of the choir was more important than ever. As a result, parish choirs of all kinds now flourish, from versatile groups that sing a broad range of musical styles to more specialized groups, such as Gospel choirs, chant ensembles, and LifeTeen bands. Many parishes have several choirs, including a "traditional" choir, "contemporary" ensemble, youth choir, children's choir, and funeral choir.

A closer reading of church documents on music in the liturgy is gradually changing the way choirs and other music ministers interact with the larger assembly. Official church documents, including the recent Revised General Instruction of the Roman Missal, envision liturgical celebrations in which the assembly engages in sung dialogue with the priest and in responsive singing with the choir and cantor. The presupposition of these documents is that the liturgy is fundamentally a sung celebration, in which the assembly of the faithful, the priest, and the choir (or cantor) have active and distinct roles. Although the choir can—and should—sing alone at times, the singing of the choir should always be integral to the celebration, and always planned in relation to the singing and prayer of the entire assembly. Whatever the style, choirs face the challenge of fostering active participation by the assembly while striving for the best musical quality possible.

The Challenge of Diversity

Commentators regularly call attention to the enormous diversity of the church in the United States, especially in its cultural and ethnic composition. Pastoral musicians serving dioceses and national organizations confront this every time they plan a large event.

How do music ministers plan for music that will allow all to sing with one voice, while respecting and affirming the variety of cultural voices within the church? Should we all sing some parts of the liturgy in Latin to draw us together? Should we all sing in Spanish, Vietnamese, Creole, and English at the same celebration? Should different languages be used for different parts? How, and to what extent, should the musical styles of various cultural groups be incorporated into large-scale liturgical celebrations? Who decides what constitutes a "genuine" Hispanic or African-American style?

Parish musicians often deal not only with a variety of cultural backgrounds, but also with various age groups and musical tastes. Many parishes provide a smorgasbord of liturgical musical choices, using different styles of music at different Sunday Masses. It is not uncommon for parishes to celebrate a youth Mass each Sunday, incorporating musical styles such as "praise music" or "Christian rock."

Some communities have rejected this approach, finding that while it addresses the variety of musical tastes, it does little to foster the unity of the parish and the ability of the whole community to sing and pray the liturgy together. In these situations, musicians are challenged to incorporate various styles into all parish celebrations and to develop music ministers capable of singing and playing in those styles.

Developing Music Ministries

Every community needs ministers of music, but different communities require different types of leadership, depending on their makeup and size. An urban cathedral or a sizable parish community may require a full-time professional music director, while a smaller urban or rural parish may have to make do with a part-time or volunteer director.

Since the Second Vatican Council, the number of full-time music directors in United States parishes has risen dramatically, especially in larger and more urban dioceses. One challenge for N.A.P.M., and other national organizations, academic institutions, and diocesan offices, is to provide the programs needed for music leaders in all nineteen thousand Catholic parishes in the United States. Of these, at least a thousand Latin-rite parishes in the United States currently have full-time directors. However, in many cases the music director is also responsible for some other aspect of parish life—usually liturgy for the parish or music for the school.

The need for leadership is just as crucial for good liturgical celebration in smaller parishes or those that have fewer financial resources. Many such communities are served by a part-time or volunteer music director or coordinator. With nearly three thousand rural parishes and at least that many smaller churches in cities, suburbs, and towns, there is a pressing need to find ways to help these directors to receive ongoing formation in liturgical studies, musical skills, and pastoral ministry.

Directors and coordinators of music, of course, comprise only a small percentage of the people who serve in music ministry. Many parishes also rely on paid and volunteer musicians

J. MICHAEL McMAHON   61

who serve as cantors, psalm singers, choir directors, choir singers, organists, and instrumentalists of various kinds. These ministers—hundreds of thousands of them—also require continuing formation not only in their musical roles, but also as liturgical ministers.

A surprisingly large number of parishes do not have a single person who is responsible for overall leadership in music ministry, but have separate directors in charge of each Sunday Mass. Therefore, bishops and pastors also need formation in musical matters, so they can recruit competent music ministers to coordinate this critically important aspect of pastoral ministry.

Music and Mission

Continuing formation is clearly crucial for music ministers of all kinds, because the church's music is linked so strongly to the life of the community as it forms its members to carry on the mission of Christ. To join in the song of the liturgy is to make a commitment to the mystery of Christ that we celebrate. Participation in the liturgy of word and sacrament is intimately linked to participation in what Karl Rahner, SJ, called the "liturgy of the world." Even as music evokes the presence and power of God through its beauty, the active singing of God's people makes them sharers in the mission of Christ to serve and to witness.

Ministers of Communion

Margaret Mary Kelleher, OSU

Margaret Mary Kelleher, OSU, is associate professor in the School of Theology and Religious Studies at The Catholic University of America in Washington, D.C.

Someone once asked me, "Why do we need ministers of Communion? Why not just pass around the eucharistic bread and wine, and let people take it themselves?"

There are several answers. For one thing, a large Sunday assembly gathered in a parish church needs order in the assembly and reverence for the mystery being celebrated, and that calls for the use of ministers. I once visited a parish where, for practical reasons, part of the assembly passed the plate of hosts from one to another without any verbal interaction. For me, it was a totally impersonal experience; I had no sense of being part of the corporate Body of Christ.

But the primary reason for having eucharistic ministers is a theological one, delineated especially well by St. Paul and St. Augustine. The Eucharist is a gift to be given and received. The ritual interaction between the giver and receiver is an expression of the communion that lies at the heart of the church's identity. But, although this is the fundamental reason, it does not appear to be the primary value in the official rubrics concerning Holy Communion.

These directives indicate that, while everyone in the assembly who is not a priest must receive Communion, the presiding priest himself must take the eucharistic bread and cup at the altar, receiving from no one. Thus, the official rubrics seem to support the hierarchical ordering of the assembly, with its associated distinction between ordained priests and the rest of the baptized.

Some Historical Background

We do not know who distributed the eucharistic bread and wine when first-century Christian communities gathered to celebrate the Lord's Supper. Several documents from the second, third, and fourth centuries refer to bread and wine being distributed by bishops, presbyters, and deacons, but it also seems to have been ordinary practice for lay members of the assembly to take some of the eucharistic bread home with them. While this would be given to those who were sick or dying, laypeople would also sometimes self-communicate on weekdays. Though legislation forbidding laypersons to act as ministers of Communion began appearing during the seventh century, the practice of the laity bringing the Eucharist to the sick continued in some places for centuries. As early as the ninth century, related legislation appeared restricting laypeople from baking the bread for the Eucharist, receiving it in their hands, and having access to the cup.

For centuries, the church's liturgical practice evinced no memory of a time when all the baptized were allowed to serve as ministers of Communion. This began to change, however, in the years following the Second Vatican Council. During the 1960s and early 1970s, bishops from the United States and other countries received permission from Rome to permit laypeople to administer Communion in certain situations when there was a scarcity of ordained ministers.

The practice of allowing lay ministers of Communion to serve at the parish eucharistic assembly, and of having special ministers bring Communion to parishioners who were unable to attend Sunday Mass, spread rapidly in the United States. Around this time, I was working in a large urban parish that had many elderly people who were unable to attend Sunday Mass. Many parishioners volunteered to become ministers of Communion, and after a time of preparation, began to bring Communion to homebound parishioners. As a result of this ministry, countless numbers of the sick and elderly were ritually reconnected to the Sunday worship.

The Ritual Enactment of Communion

In every celebration of the Eucharist, the Lord's Prayer, the rite of peace, and the breaking of the eucharistic bread all lead to the ritual climax of Communion: the assembly's sharing in the body and blood of Christ. And the way this ritual is enacted can either support or detract from a vision of ecclesial communion. The movement and arrangement of persons within the space, the sequence of actions and the words, both spoken and sung, all shape this vision. Since assemblies and church buildings are quite diverse, it is important that people in local assemblies reflect on their present practice and carefully choreograph the flow of the ritual.

I remember the Sunday worship of one congregation at which the altar stood in the center of the assembly. At Communion time, eucharistic ministers took up their stations on each of the four sides of the altar. This arrangement allowed the congregation to have the experience of truly being an assembly gathered around the table of the Lord. But I also participated in a Sunday Mass in a parish where the opposite occurred. In this church, half the ministers of Communion were stationed at the entrance of the building, so that half the congregation had to turn and walk away from the altar in order to receive Communion. After this experience, I made sure to sit in the front half of the church, so that I would never again have to turn my back on the altar. Care also should be taken to ensure a sufficient number of ministers of the cup (as well as to ensure that they do not stand too close to the ministers of the eucharistic bread). This will ensure that the Communion procession moves in a dignified and reverent manner.

Official instructions regarding extraordinary ministers of Communion in the United States have varied since the practice was first allowed. In 1973, they were told to enter the sanctuary and stand near the altar during the breaking of the bread. In 1985, a directory setting out practices for Communion under both kinds allowed extraordinary ministers to assist the presiding bishop or priest in breaking the bread and pouring the wine into the chalices if priests, deacons, and acolytes were not available. But in 2002, Norms for the Distribution and Reception of Holy Communion under Both Kinds in the Dioceses of the United States of America was issued, restricting the breaking of the bread and the pouring of the wine to the ordained. Extraordinary ministers are now to approach the altar as the priest receives Communion, then to receive Communion from the priest and to accept from him the sacred vessels for distributing Communion to the faithful.

Unfortunately, this directive is being interpreted in a narrow way in some local assemblies. Since the altar stands within the sanctuary space, there is no reason that lay ministers of Communion cannot enter the sanctuary area before the priest's Communion (as many have become accustomed to doing).

In deciding where to place the ministers, consideration should also be given to the arrangement of people within the space, so that the Body of Christ appears as an organic unity. In one parish I saw a contradictory image created when the ministers of Communion stood across the entrance of the sanctuary with their backs to the rest of the congregation as the presiding priest received Communion. They formed a human wall blocking the assembly's view of the altar. Instead of feeling included in what was taking place at the altar, I felt excluded.

One instruction that has remained consistent tells ministers of Communion what to say when they offer the eucharistic bread and wine. When offering the bread (or cup), the minister is to say, "The body [or blood] of Christ," and the recipient is to say, "Amen." At times I have encountered eucharistic ministers who do not follow this instruction, instead saying, "This is the body of Christ." Such a statement reduces the multiple levels of meaning in the prescribed phrase. As St. Augustine taught, saying "Amen" to this declaration allows one to express belief in the presence of Christ in the Eucharist, to affirm one's identity as a member of the Body of Christ, and to commit oneself to live as a member of that body.

Acting as the Body of Christ

Liturgy is ecclesial action, and the church is disclosed and shaped in the ritual action of local assemblies. In those liturgies we see who we are and who we are called to be. The wonderful service of lay ministers of Communion within and outside of Mass can provide some illustrations of this. Thirty years ago, I worked in a parish where one new eucharistic minister brought Communion to an elderly woman and discovered that she had no one to do regular grocery shopping for her. Thus began a family ministry, in which the eucharistic minister, as well as her husband and children, took turns shopping and visiting this parishioner. They beautifully expressed and extended what St. Paul called, the *koinonia,* or shared community, that bound them together in the Body of Christ.

A former graduate student of mine researched the experience of lay ministers who brought Communion to patients in a local hospital. She told the story of a woman who had a rather dramatic personal experience as she was giving Communion to a patient. The lay minister confided that as she was saying, "The body of Christ," she felt, for the first time, a strong sense of herself and others as actual members of that body. Clearly, the performance of this ritual action had altered her personal and ecclesial identity.

The fact that women serve within and beyond the assembly as ministers of Communion is one of the most positive outcomes of the practice of allowing the laity to participate in this ministry. I remember how moving it was to have my own sister serve as a minister of the cup during the Mass in which we celebrated the twenty-fifth anniversary of my final profession of vows as a religious, something that would have been unheard of thirty years earlier, at my first profession.

In addition to inviting women into a ministry associated with the altar, the practice of having laypersons serve as ministers has allowed us to manifest the diversity of bodies that make up the corporate body of Christ. The parish in which I now regularly worship is comprised of people from a great variety of countries and cultural backgrounds. Each Sunday, some of this diversity is evident in those laypersons who serve the assembly as ministers of Communion. It is an impressive illustration of the diversity—the catholicity—that is a characteristic of the Body of Christ.

Ritual action often provides a context for the negotiation of relationships within a social body, and liturgy is no exception. In the years since Vatican II, liturgy has provided a significant arena for the church's negotiation of its renewed self-understanding as a corporate body enlivened by the Spirit of Christ. Is it "ordinary" or "extraordinary" for baptized members of this body to serve as ministers of Communion? On the one hand, the ritual norms have consistently identified the role of lay ministers of Communion as extraordinary, and the recent restrictions placed on their activities at the altar reinforce the distinction between the ministry of the ordained and that of the laity. On the other hand, the ritual practice of the church in the United States for the past thirty years suggests that the service of lay ministers is quite ordinary. At issue, and subject to further negotiation, of course, is the role of the baptized within the corporate body of Christ.

Paul and Augustine on the Great Mystery

By way of concluding, let me return to St. Paul and St. Augustine. Early in the fifth century, Augustine, bishop of Hippo, delivered a sermon in which he instructed the newly baptized about the meaning of the Eucharist:

> What you see . . . is bread and a cup. This is what your eyes report to you. But your faith has need to be taught that the bread is the body of Christ, the cup the blood of Christ. . . . If, then, you wish to understand the body of Christ, listen to the Apostle as he says to the faithful, "You are the body of Christ and his members." . . . You reply, "Amen," to that which you are, and by replying you consent. For you hear, "The body of Christ," and you reply, "Amen." Be a member of the body of Christ so that your "Amen" may be true. . . . Be what you see, and receive what you are. (Sermon 272)

I offer this quotation because of what I have learned from many years of teaching graduate and undergraduate students and giving talks on the Eucharist in a variety of parishes. When I ask people what they are doing when they say, "Amen," in response to, "The body of Christ," they often say that they are expressing faith in the presence of Christ in the Eucharist. Yet I never hear them say that they are affirming their identity as members of the body of Christ.

When I read Augustine's sermon to them, it usually comes as a surprise. St. Paul wrote to the church at Corinth that "we were all baptized into one body—Jews or Greeks, slaves or free—and were all made to drink of one Spirit" (1 Cor 12:13). It was the shared gift of the Spirit that made the Corinthians one body. That same baptismal gift has continued to be constitutive of the church through the centuries. The gift of the Spirit, given in baptism, incorporates people into the body of Christ, where they participate or share in Christ's life. As I have noted, Paul used the word *koinonia* to describe this shared life, the communion of persons with Christ and with one another. Members of the body of Christ are a communion in Christ's Spirit.

In his letters, Paul made it clear that the gift of *koinonia* was a dynamic reality, a gift to be realized continually within the Body of Christ. At times he called upon the churches to express their shared life in Christ by contributing to a collection that would alleviate the sufferings of members of a church in another locale. His rationale was that those who had come to share in one another's spiritual blessings ought to be of service to one another in material things (Rom 15:25–27). The communion in Christ's Spirit, at the heart of the community's identity as the body of Christ, was regularly expressed and realized each time the church gathered to celebrate the Lord's Supper.

As Paul reminded the Corinthians, "[T]he cup of blessing that we bless, is it not a sharing in the blood of Christ? The bread that we break, is it not a sharing in the body of Christ? Because there is one bread, we who are many are one body, for we all partake of the one bread" (1 Cor 10:16–17). Paul's reminder to the church of Corinth continues to be pertinent for every liturgical assembly gathered to celebrate the Eucharist and to share in the body and blood of Christ. The eucharistic ritual action of each assembly is intended to be a manifestation and realization of its shared life in Christ.

The Ministry of Hospitality

Thomas Richstatter, OFM

Thomas Richstatter, OFM, is professor of theology at St. Meinrad's Seminary, St. Meinrad, Indiana.

*I*t can be lonely living by oneself in a small town, as I do. But I can always go to Wal-Mart and know that I will be met at the door by a smiling employee who will greet me with, "Welcome to Wal-Mart," and give me a shopping cart and a flyer with today's specials. If only I could be so lucky at church! How many times have I gone to Sunday Mass and opened the church door to find myself in a dark vestibule, greeted only by lost gloves, mismatched galoshes, and a stack of collection baskets.

Thanks be to God, this is no longer the case in most Catholic parishes. Today we are greeted at the door by ministers of hospitality, who welcome us into the eucharistic assembly. But it was not too many years ago when, if you found yourself greeted at the church door by a minister of hospitality, you knew you were in a Protestant church.

The minister of hospitality (or greeter) is a relatively new role for Catholics. Pre-Vatican II editions of the Roman Missal contain no mention of lay greeters. The words *hospitality* and *greeter* are not found in Sacrosanctum Concilium. The General Instruction of the Roman Missal lists among the liturgical ministers, "those who, in some places, meet the faithful at the church entrance, lead them to appropriate places, and direct processions," but no name is given to this ministry, nor is it described in any further detail. The current edition of the General Instruction mentions this ministry at the very end of the list of liturgical ministries, following "those who take up the collection in church."

Understanding a "New" Ministry

The Introduction to the Order of Mass, published in 2003 by the U.S. Bishops' Committee on the Liturgy as a pastoral resource, quotes St. Paul's instruction to the Romans to "Welcome one another, therefore, just as Christ has welcomed you" (Rom 15:7). It then assigns to the ushers the task of "welcoming people at the door, providing them with all necessary books and aids, and helping them find their places."

Those entrusted with the task of preparing Catholics to exercise the various ministries at Sunday Eucharist might argue that greeters and ushers are distinct ministries. Or perhaps those who have traditionally served as ushers—taking up the collection and counting the money—need additional formation to serve as ministers of hospitality.

How does one prepare for this ministry? Can hospitality be learned? Does one take a course for greeters at Wal-Mart? Obviously, there are certain facts and skills that can be learned easily: when to arrive, what to do if someone becomes ill, where the bulletins are kept, and the like.

It is more difficult to develop a sense of this ministry. All the various liturgical ministers must work together toward a common goal. One minister does not seat people while another minister is proclaiming the Scriptures. Assisting with the Communion procession is different from simply directing traffic.

More difficult yet is teaching the deeper issues: Why are we doing this in the first place? What purpose does welcoming serve? Why do we feel we need this ministry now, when we got by for so many years without it?

Perhaps one reason Catholics did not feel the need to welcome people coming to Sunday Mass was that we had been taught we "had to go." Inviting Catholics to Sunday Mass was simply unnecessary—like the U.S. Government "inviting" you to pay income tax: you do it or else! For some, obligation may still be the primary motivation for attending Mass. After publishing an article on "Why I Go to Mass," I received a letter informing me that "the reasons given in the article are all right, I guess; but you didn't mention the main reason we go to Mass. We'll rot in hell if we don't!"

Today we have to do more than threaten; we have to invite and welcome. The U.S. bishops, in their "Message to Young Adults" in 1995, state: "We acknowledge the pain many of you speak of in feeling unwelcome and alone—strangers in the house of God." The bishops apologize for past failures to extend hospitality and express their hope that in the future, "anyone who enters a Catholic church for Mass, or at any other time, will feel comfortable and welcome."

Welcoming and hospitality become important whenever we need to do something together. But the Mass was something we once did alone. Only recently have we come to understand the Eucharist as a communal act. During my high-school and college years, I went to Mass "to pray." I said my prayers, and the priest said his. I was "talking to God" about my life and my concerns; the priest was "saying Mass." I prayed quietly in English; the priest prayed in Latin. If there were other people in church at the same time—five or five hundred—they did not concern me; they said their prayers, and I said mine.

I believe this is still the experience of many Catholics. The Mass is not yet perceived to be something that we do together. A few years ago, during the question period following a presentation I gave on the "new" liturgy, a gentleman asked me: "Father, why do I have to turn and shake hands and give that 'kiss of peace' before Holy Communion? It's a terrible distraction. I don't know those people. And the ones I know, I don't even like."

It has been forty years since the Second Vatican Council wrote: "Liturgical services are not private functions, but are celebrations of the church . . . liturgical services pertain to the whole body of the church" (Sacrosanctum Concilium, No. 26). This was a revolutionary insight. It changes everything. Mass is not a private devotion. We, as church, are doing something together. And the priest is not doing "his thing" up front, far away; he is presiding, coordinating, and leading the community.

Changing people's understanding of Mass from a private prayer to a communal act is made more difficult by the fact that, as Americans, we tend to think of "religion" as something private and individual. Charles Lippy, in his study of popular religiosity in the United States, *Being Religious American Style,* concludes: "Being religious, American style, is to share in that dynamic, but highly personal and ultimately very private, enterprise of endowing one's own life with meaning." Sunday Mass, for many Catholics, continues to be a "highly personal and ultimately very private enterprise." This makes hospitality and welcoming both more difficult and all the more necessary.

A Catholic Welcome

What can we do to show that the Eucharist is a communal activity? Greeting people at the door is a start. It alerts us to the fact that we are going to do something with others. "Welcome" implies "I am happy that you have come." The first impression a visitor receives is extremely important. But hospitality is everybody's ministry.

We practice hospitality in choosing where we sit. Do we take the aisle seat and block access to the rest of the pew or chairs? Are those who come after us forced to crawl over us to find a place? What does it say to latecomers when the only open places are way up front? And how do we acknowledge the presence of those who come in and sit next to us? Hospitality is not restricted to the ministers at the church door.

It is also helpful if we think of the first part of the Mass as "gathering rites," rather than "introductory rites" or "entrance rites," because "gathering" names the purpose of these actions and prayers: "to ensure that the faithful who come together as one establish communion" (General Instruction, No. 46). We exercise the ministry of hospitality when we pick up the service book and sing the gathering hymn. If we actually are doing something together, we should look like it.

We also practice hospitality when we open our minds and hearts to the proclamation of the Scriptures. When we listen to the psalm refrain and repeat it back as best we can, even if the melody is new, we are honing our listening skills and training our ears to hear the word of God. And this word, received in the Holy Spirit, broadens our understanding of whom we must welcome into our parish assembly. The U.S. bishops' 2001 document, "Built of Living Stones," underlines this idea: "The Gospel requires that particular care be taken to welcome into the church's assembly those often discarded by society—the socially and economically marginalized, the elderly, the sick, those with disabilities, and those with special needs" (No. 42). The General Intercessions expand the horizons of our prayer.

Understanding the Eucharist as sharing a meal together, rather than "receiving Holy Communion," lies at the heart of this communal understanding of the Mass. Those parishes where the liturgical assembly is a real community must take special care to welcome visitors. A stranger should be able to enter a church and feel perfectly at home. But when you enter a gathering that has a real feeling of community, you may feel out of place unless you are welcomed. I have lived in parishes where we had to be continually reminded to welcome visitors, lest they get the impression that we were some sort of "clique." The feeling of community was that palpable.

I have found some Catholics who think this whole "welcoming" business is destroying our traditional sense of reverence and replacing it with some folksy, feel-good experience. This is a false conclusion. If you wish to invite a guest into your home, you must have space. You have to "make room." To invite others into our hearts and our worship, we must make room for them. The enemy of reverence is not hospitality but arrogance. If we wish to worship in an atmosphere of reverence, we must rid our churches, our congregations, and our hearts of any superfluous self-importance, pride, and ambition that might be filling up our "guest spaces." We must empty ourselves in order to make room for the other to enter in. This is the difficult part of hospitality.

Arrogance and all that goes with it need to be "sacrificed" at the Eucharist. When we are weighed down with pride and self-importance, it is difficult to mount the cross with Jesus, who "humbled himself and became obedient to the point of death—even death on a cross" (Phil 2:8). Emptying ourselves of arrogance is the key to experiencing reverence.

At a recent meeting of the North American Academy of Liturgy, the study group of which I was a member visited a parish in Harlem for Sunday Eucharist. After Mass a group of parishioners met with us to discuss our experience. One of our group asked the parishioners, "When do you have your deepest experience of prayer? Where in the liturgy do you experience God?" Without hesitation, several of the parishioners replied:

"In the welcoming community." Hospitality is a doorway to transcendence.

The ministry of hospitality that we exercise at the Eucharist is not simply a sales device. It must be the liturgical enactment of the hospitality that permeates our daily living. Hospitality is not an add-on; for the Christian, it is the bottom line: "Then the king will say to those at his right hand, 'Come, you that are blessed by my Father, inherit the kingdom prepared for you from the foundation of the world; for I was hungry and you gave me food, I was thirsty and you gave me something to drink, I was a stranger and you welcomed me'" (Mt 25:34–35).

Celebrating "Good Liturgy"

Nathan D. Mitchell

Nathan D. Mitchell is associate director for research at the Center for Pastoral Liturgy at the University of Notre Dame, Notre Dame, Indiana.

What makes "good liturgy"? That is the question with which a squad of talented Catholic liturgists have been wrestling throughout these last nine chapters. Beginning with the most basic liturgical minister of all—the assembly—these men and women have probed the arts of presiding and preaching; the roles of deacons, lectors, eucharistic ministers, music ministers, and parish liturgy committees; and finally, hospitality, "everyone's ministry." Several themes have surfaced in these thoughtful essays: the ritual readiness of the assembly, the need for care and competence in celebration, the twin tables of word and sacrament, communal sung prayer as a worshipful response to God, the essential link between liturgy and social justice, Communion as *koinonia,* a holy living together in faith, through Christ and the Spirit—and finally, the joyful enthusiasm that erupts when humble service unites presider and participants.

Starting from Experience

My task is to revisit this question a final time: What makes good liturgy? In seeking an answer, surely experience is the best place to begin. So let me start with two extraordinary examples—one recent; the other, from a few years ago.

Last year, on the Second Sunday of Lent, I had the pleasure of joining the parish community of St. Mark's, in Independence, Missouri, as it celebrated the dedication of a new church. Located in a rapidly growing suburb of Kansas City, the parish had literally outgrown its worship space. Thanks to lively collaboration between pastor and parishioners, a sound planning program had been put in place, artists and architects hired, and ground broken. Today a once-muddy field has become the site of a magnificent, Romanesque-style, cruciform structure that, in spite of its traditional form, allows the assembly to gather in a semicircle around the altar. Sightlines are unobstructed, all lighting is indirect (no "hanging jungle" of cords and lamp fixtures), the floor slopes gently toward altar and ambo, and worshipers with disabilities are fully accommodated.

The dedication liturgy was celebrated on a sunny Sunday as a late Midwestern winter was struggling into spring, breeding hope out of thawing soil. Nearly a thousand worshipers packed the church for a rarely performed rite that consists chiefly in the solemn baptism of the building, with water flung in every direction, and crosses traced with chrism on its walls. As the long liturgy unfolded, it was clear that the parishioners and the bishop loved what they were doing together. People sang robustly in several languages, supported by adult and children's choirs, and accompanied by handbells, organ, piano, guitars, and percussion. As the bishop doffed his chasuble, rolled up the sleeves of his alb, and began slathering consecrated oil over the surface of the red-oak altar, the assembly's interest quickened. Then, from each direction, small groups of parishioners advanced toward the altar, dancing a solemn saraband. Their arms were outstretched, holding censers, lights, and freshly laundered linens for wiping and drying the wood of the altar/cross/body of Christ.

Slowly the space became suffused with smoke, a prelude to the fires the bishop would soon set on the altar as part of the dedication ritual. One could not help imagining the spice-bearing women approaching Jesus' tomb "on the first day of the week"—or even the recent photos from the Hubble telescope that show swirling galaxies, star nurseries, and spirals of incandescent gas glowing in the first moments of creation. The liturgy lasted for hours, but time flew. I overheard one parishioner say as she left church, "That was the shortest three hours I ever spent!"

Led by their bishop, the baptized Body of Christ that meets at St. Mark's had baptized their new worship space. Was it "good liturgy?" You bet. Careful planning, loving attention to ritual detail, enthusiastic singing, and participation by everyone made the celebration memorable. It was a superb example of what happens when parishes take to heart the principles of the Second Vatican Council's Sacrosanctum Concilium, and when they let the speech, song, silence, and symbols of a renewed rite speak with fullness and authority. (It helped that the pastor and his staff had provided good liturgical catechesis for the parish prior to the celebration.)

My second example comes from a few summers back, when I was a guest at St. Augustine's parish in Louisville, Kentucky, an inner-city, historically African-American community, whose roots stretch back to the nineteenth century. The people, presider, ministers, and musicians had undoubtedly planned the liturgy for this Sunday in Ordinary Time, but what impressed me was that all the worshipers knew "in their bones" how to do the liturgical act—how to do it from memory, with dignity and grace, naturally, unhurriedly, welcoming the stranger in their midst. Though everyone participated vigorously, no one (except me) found it necessary to refer to hymnals, missalettes, or other "worship aids." It amazed me that almost the entire Mass, from entrance rite to dismissal, was sung. The homily was punctuated by acclamation and chanted exchanges between presider and people. Three different choirs (children, teenagers, adults) supported the congregation's singing, much of it rhythmically and melodically complex, yet quite singable.

There was literally standing room only in the cramped upstairs room where the people of St. Augustine's celebrate the Eucharist (the frame church's lower level is used for the dinners that typically follow Sunday liturgy). Yet hospitable accommodations were made. In one area toward the rear of the room sat some people to whom everyone seemed to defer as community elders, most of them women advanced in age. I was reminded of a similar group at a parish in the diocese of Oakland, California, where each lady elder was invariably addressed by the respectful title "Mama." One of them, Mama Camille, had quite a reputation for wit. Stopping to chat with her one Sunday morning, a parishioner asked, "How're you doin' today, Mama Camille?" Mama pondered a moment before replying, "I'm somewhere between, 'Thank you, Jesus,' and 'Lord, have mercy!'"

Respect for each person's gift and ministry, generous hospitality, honoring the community's elders—all were palpable as St. Augustine's parishioners celebrated their liturgy. It was definitely their liturgy; yet at the same time, it was unmistakably the Roman rite, shaped, as Vatican II recommends in the Sacrosanctum Concilium, to embrace the distinctive culture of that community (Nos. 37–38). Our Mass had begun at ten o'clock. By midafternoon, people were still chatting over dinner in the church basement, and a small army of volunteers had gathered in the rectory to make soup and sandwiches. (St. Augustine's kitchen is well known to the poor and homeless of the neighborhood.)

Was this "good liturgy?" You bet. I have often thought that if Blessed Pope John XXIII could somehow be present to celebrate with communities such as St. Mark's and St. Augustine's, Sunday after Sunday, he would come away glowing, happy with his legacy, his heart singing "a song of the brightness of water" (the title of one of Pope John Paul II's poems). He would, I think, recognize the Roman rite, adapted, as the liturgy constitution insists, to the "qualities and talents" of diverse peoples (No. 37). He would acknowledge their differences and welcome them. He would embrace their music with enthusiasm. He would grasp how much the liturgy means to these people, how precious a gift it is, how deeply it supports their common life. He would see what a legacy of worthy celebration they hope to leave their children. He would see the Body of Christ stretching out its hands to those who have been shut up and shut out. And he would be reminded that in the midst of that meal the night before he died, Jesus was the one kneeling, with a bowl of dirty water in his hands.

What Makes Liturgy "Good"?

Comparing these experiences to the wonderful essays in this book, I find a set of common characteristics. I suggest, therefore, that good liturgy results when:

- Vigorous popular participation is encouraged and enhanced by presiders whose style is "strong, loving, and wise," rather than tentative, domineering, or disengaged.

- Worshipers can see, hear, and join in the liturgical action, since at Mass the people not only offer the sacrifice through the priest's hands; they offer it together with him, and include themselves in the offering.

- A rich diversity of ministers do all and only those tasks that belong to them (this applies to presiders as well).

- Both the "vertical" and "horizontal" axes of Christian worship are respected—that is, the assembly's focus deepens its prayer while heightening its reverence for everyone in the assembly, especially the least and littlest.

- Reverence means not simply a way of behaving at Mass, but an attitude toward other people. The opposite of reverence is arrogance and a refusal to greet with awe those persons and things that are higher than oneself.

- Ritual spaces provide sufficient breathing room for participants. For Christian liturgy, despite its occasional wordiness, shares something vital in common with silence: both are open spaces where God can address us in the first person.

- Preachers are poets, not exegetes, pundits, or comedians. For the preacher's task is to let the word speak through the mercy of the body, to find the memorable image that enables the assembly to name the grace that suffuses both world and worship.

- The ritual readiness of participants is made possible by rites that are so sturdy, stable, and familiar that, far from inspiring complacency, they challenge a community to embrace the tough work of conversion.

- The sacramental celebration comforts the uncomfortable and discomfits the comfortable.

- The community eschews self-righteous rubricism, yet avoids the temptation to make the rite up as it goes along—a strategy that inevitably impedes participation, because people do not know what will happen next.

- The community's diversity (cultural, racial, linguistic, generational, etc.) is joyfully acknowledged rather than painfully sidestepped or ignored.

- Ritual spaces are so situated in neighborhoods that their symbolic presence as the house of God's holy people is obvious, that they can accommodate the movement of people during the liturgy (e.g., at Communion), and that the essential relation between liturgy and justice, ethics and Eucharist, is clear.

- Christians remember that the Eucharist commits us to the poor and that we cannot truly receive Christ's body and blood unless we come to recognize Christ in the poorest among us.

Always in Paradise

My list is not complete, nor will its content surprise anyone who has been working in the field of pastoral liturgy in the past forty years. It concludes with a reminder that what Pope John Paul II has called "the option for the poor" is actually a eucharistic obligation for Christians. As St. John Chrysostom once warned us, it does us no good to adorn and adore Christ's body in church if we fail to recognize Christ's body when it stands outside, hungry, and neglected. Liturgy is the language the Catholic community speaks when it is at home, and it is most at home when it is worshiping God and serving the poor.

When asked one time whether the poet William Blake was at home, his wife Catherine replied, "I see very little of Mr. Blake;

you see, he is always in paradise." At home, we Catholics speak of paradise while holding a bowl of dirty water in our hands. We come to the liturgy not to see our own desires made lucid, but to see a reflection of ecstasy at its most difficult—in the cross that speaks, always calling us to service, faith, and repentance.

Selections from
❀ Sacrosanctum ❀
Concilium

*I*t was no accident that the first document published by the Second Vatican Council, on December 4, 1963, was Sacrosanctum Concilium, ("The Constitution of the Sacred Liturgy"), for the updating of the liturgy was at the heart of the general reforms of Vatican II. Many of the essays in this book refer frequently to this publication, which still serves as the guiding light for anyone interested in serious study of the liturgy. And like the best of the Council's work, Sacrosanctum Concilium represents not only an important historical document, but also an opportunity for personal prayer and reflection. (The Arabic numerals denote verbatim citations from S.C.)

The Goals of the Council

1. This sacred Council has several aims in view: it desires to impart an ever-increasing vigor to the Christian life of the faithful; to adapt more suitably to the needs of our own times those institutions which are subject to change; to foster whatever can promote union among all who believe in Christ; to strengthen whatever can help to call the whole of mankind into the household of the church. The Council therefore sees particularly cogent reasons for undertaking the reform and promotion of the liturgy.

The Faithful Express Their Lives in the Liturgy

2. For the liturgy, "through which the work of our redemption is accomplished,"[1] most of all in the divine sacrifice of the Eucharist, is the outstanding means whereby the faithful may express in their lives, and manifest to others, the mystery of Christ and the real nature of the true church. It is of the essence of the church that she be both human and divine, visible and yet invisibly equipped, eager to act and yet intent on contemplation, present in this world and yet not at home in it; and she is all these things in such wise that in her the human is directed and subordinated to the divine, the visible likewise to the invisible, action to contemplation, and this present world to that city yet to come, which we seek. While the liturgy daily builds up those who are within into a holy temple of the Lord, into a dwelling place for God in the Spirit, to the mature measure of the fullness of Christ, at the same time it marvelously strengthens their power to preach Christ, and thus shows forth the church to those who are outside as a sign lifted up among the nations under which the scattered children of God may be gathered together, until there is one sheepfold and one shepherd.

Christ's Presence in the Mass

7. To accomplish so great a work, Christ is always present in his church, especially in her liturgical celebrations. He is present in the sacrifice of the Mass, not only in the person of his minister, "the same now offering, through the ministry of priests, who formerly offered himself on the cross,"[2] but especially under the eucharistic species. By his power he is present in the sacraments, so that when a man baptizes it is really Christ himself who baptizes. He is present in his word, since it is he himself who speaks when the holy scriptures are read in the church. He is present, lastly, when the church prays and sings, for he promised: "Where

two or three are gathered together in my name, there am I in the midst of them" (Mt 18:20).

Christ indeed always associates the church with himself in this great work wherein God is perfectly glorified and men and women are sanctified. The church is his beloved bride who calls to her Lord, and through him offers worship to the Eternal Father.

Rightly, then, the liturgy is considered as an exercise of the priestly office of Jesus Christ. In the liturgy the sanctification of mankind is signified by signs perceptible to the senses, and is effected in a way which corresponds with each of these signs; in the liturgy the whole public worship is performed by the Mystical Body of Jesus Christ, that is, by the head and his members.

From this it follows that every liturgical celebration, because it is an action of Christ the priest and of his Body which is the church, is a sacred action surpassing all others; no other action of the church can equal its efficacy by the same title and to the same degree.

A Foretaste of Heaven

8. In the earthly liturgy we take part in a foretaste of that heavenly liturgy which is celebrated in the holy city of Jerusalem toward which we journey as pilgrims, where Christ is sitting at the right hand of God, a minister of the sanctuary and of the true tabernacle; we sing a hymn to the Lord's glory with all the warriors of the heavenly army; venerating the memory of the saints, we hope for some part and fellowship with them; we eagerly await the Savior, Our Lord Jesus Christ, until he, our life, shall appear and we too will appear with him in glory.

The Summit of the Church's Activity

10. Nevertheless the liturgy is the summit toward which the activity of the church is directed; at the same time it is the font

from which all her power flows. For the aim and object of apostolic works is that all who are made children of God by faith and baptism should come together to praise God in the midst of his church, to take part in the sacrifice, and to eat the Lord's Supper.

The liturgy in its turn moves the faithful, filled with "the paschal sacraments," to be "one in holiness" [3]; it prays that "they may hold fast in their lives to what they have grasped by their faith;" the renewal in the Eucharist of the covenant between the Lord and humanity draws the faithful into the compelling love of Christ and sets them on fire. From the liturgy, therefore, and especially from the Eucharist, as from a font, grace is poured forth upon us; and the sanctification of men and women in Christ and the glorification of God, to which all other activities of the church are directed as toward their end, is achieved in the most efficacious way possible.

Active Engagement by the Faithful

11. But in order that the liturgy may be able to produce its full effects, it is necessary that the faithful come to it with proper dispositions, that their minds should be attuned to their voices, and that they should cooperate with divine grace lest they receive it in vain. Pastors of souls must therefore realize that, when the liturgy is celebrated, something more is required than the mere observation of the laws governing valid and licit celebration; it is their duty also to ensure that the faithful take part fully aware of what they are doing, actively engaged in the rite, and enriched by its effects.

Full, Conscious, and Active Participation

14. Mother Church earnestly desires that all the faithful should be led to that full, conscious, and active participation in liturgical

celebrations which is demanded by the very nature of the liturgy. Such participation by the Christian people as "a chosen race, a royal priesthood, a holy nation, a redeemed people" (1 Pt 2:9; cf. 2:4–5), is their right and duty by reason of their baptism.

In the restoration and promotion of the sacred liturgy, this full and active participation by all the people is the aim to be considered before all else; for it is the primary and indispensable source from which the faithful are to derive the true Christian spirit; and, therefore, pastors of souls must zealously strive to achieve it, by means of the necessary instruction, in all their pastoral work.

Yet it would be futile to entertain any hopes of realizing this unless the pastors themselves, in the first place, become thoroughly imbued with the spirit and power of the liturgy, and undertake to give instruction about it. A prime need, therefore, is that attention be directed, first of all, to the liturgical instruction of the clergy.

The Centrality of Scripture

24. Sacred Scripture is of the greatest importance in the celebration of the liturgy. For it is from Scripture that lessons are read and explained in the homily, and psalms are sung; the prayers, collects, and liturgical songs are scriptural in their inspiration and their force, and it is from the Scriptures that actions and signs derive their meaning. Thus to achieve the restoration, progress, and adaptation of the sacred liturgy, it is essential to promote that warm and living love for Scripture to which the venerable tradition of both Eastern and Western rites gives testimony.

The Sacrament of Unity

26. Liturgical services are not private functions, but are celebrations of the church, which is the "sacrament of unity," [4] namely, the holy people united and ordered under their bishops. Therefore

liturgical services pertain to the whole body of the church; they manifest it and have effects upon it; but they concern the individual members of the church in different ways, according to their differing rank, office, and actual participation.

Genuine Liturgical Functioning

29. Servers, lectors, commentators, and members of the choir also exercise a genuine liturgical function. They ought, therefore, to discharge their office with the sincere piety and decorum demanded by so exalted a ministry and rightly expected of them by God's people.

Consequently, they must all be deeply imbued with the spirit of the liturgy, each in his own measure, and they must be trained to perform their functions in a correct and orderly manner.

The Presider and the Assembly

33. Although the sacred liturgy is above all things the worship of the divine majesty, it likewise contains much instruction for the faithful. For in the liturgy God speaks to his people, and Christ is still proclaiming his gospel. And the people reply to God both by song and prayer.

Moreover, the prayers addressed to God by the priest who presides over the assembly in the person of Christ are said in the name of the entire holy people and of all present. And the visible signs used by the liturgy to signify invisible divine things have been chosen by Christ or the church. Thus not only when things are read "which were written for our instruction" (Rom 15:4), but also when the church prays or sings or acts, the faith of those taking part is nourished and their minds are raised to God, so that they may offer him their rational service and more abundantly receive his grace.

A Sacrament of Love

47. At the Last Supper, on the night when he was betrayed, our Savior instituted the eucharistic sacrifice of His Body and Blood. He did this in order to perpetuate the sacrifice of the cross throughout the centuries until he should come again, and so to entrust to his beloved spouse, the church, a memorial of his death and resurrection: a sacrament of love, a sign of unity, a bond of charity, a paschal banquet in which Christ is eaten, the mind is filled with grace, and a pledge of future glory is given to us.

The Faithful Drawn into Union with God

48. The church, therefore, earnestly desires that Christ's faithful, when present at this mystery of faith, should not be there as strangers or silent spectators; on the contrary, through a good understanding of the rites and prayers they should take part in the sacred action conscious of what they are doing, with devotion and full collaboration. They should be instructed by God's word and be nourished at the table of the Lord's body; they should give thanks to God; by offering the Immaculate Victim, not only through the hands of the priest, but also with him, they should learn also to offer themselves; through Christ the Mediator, they should be drawn day by day into ever more perfect union with God and with each other, so that, finally, God may be all in all.

The Importance of the Homily

52. By means of the homily the mysteries of the faith and the guiding principles of the Christian life are expounded from the sacred text, during the course of the liturgical year; the homily,

therefore, is to be highly esteemed as part of the liturgy itself; in fact, at those Masses which are celebrated with the assistance of the people on Sundays and feasts of obligation, it should not be omitted except for a serious reason.

The Liturgical Year

102. Holy Mother Church is conscious that she must celebrate the saving work of her divine spouse by devoutly recalling it on certain days throughout the course of the year. Every week, on the day which she has called the Lord's day, she keeps the memory of the Lord's resurrection, which she also celebrates once in the year, together with his blessed passion, in the most solemn festival of Easter.

Within the cycle of a year, moreover, she unfolds the whole mystery of Christ, from the incarnation and birth until the ascension, the day of Pentecost, and the expectation of blessed hope and of the coming of the Lord.

Recalling thus the mysteries of redemption, the church opens to the faithful the riches of her Lord's powers and merits, so that these are in some way made present for all time, and the faithful are enabled to lay hold upon them and become filled with saving grace.

The Treasure of Music

112. The musical tradition of the universal church is a treasure of inestimable value, greater even than that of any other art. The main reason for this pre-eminence is that, as sacred song united to the words, it forms a necessary or integral part of the solemn liturgy.

Holy Scripture, indeed, has bestowed praise upon sacred song, and the same may be said of the fathers of the church and of the Roman pontiffs who in recent times, led by St. Pius X, have explained more precisely the ministerial function supplied by sacred music in the service of the Lord.

Therefore, sacred music is to be considered the more holy in proportion as it is more closely connected with the liturgical action, whether it adds delight to prayer, fosters unity of minds, or confers greater solemnity upon the sacred rites. But the church approves of all forms of true art having the needed qualities, and admits them into divine worship.

Notes

1. Prayer over the offerings, ninth Sunday after Pentecost

2. Council of Trent, Session 22, September 17, 1562.

3. Post-Communion prayer

4. St. Cyprian, "On the Unity of the Catholic Church."

❦ Acknowledgments ❦

First, I would like to thank all the writers who so generously contributed to this collection. Their willingness to spend time preparing these essays, as well as their openness to revealing some personal experiences and reflections, is deeply appreciated.

Since I am no liturgical scholar, I turned to two experts who helped me to find the "right" person for each essay: James M. Schellman and Nathan D. Mitchell were enormously helpful in this regard. Thanks also to Thomas J. Reese, SJ, editor in chief of *America,* for his encouragement in the initial series, and Robert C. Collins, SJ, managing editor, for his generous assistance in the difficult (at least for me) task of translating the computer files. Casie Attardi, a wonderfully efficient editorial intern at the magazine, did the lion's share of work when it came to helping with the final edits and formatting the manuscript. As the saying goes, I couldn't have done it without her.

At Loyola Press, thanks to George Lane, SJ, and James Manney, for their early enthusiasm about this book, and to Matthew Diener for his wise advice.

Finally, I would like to thank the parish communities listed on the frontispiece of this book, for showing me, over the course of my life, how the celebration of the Mass can truly be the "source and summit" of Christian worship.

✽ About the Editor ✽

James Martin, SJ, is a Jesuit priest and associate editor of *America,* a Catholic magazine. A graduate of the University of Pennsylvania's Wharton School of Business, he worked for six years in corporate finance before entering the Society of Jesus in 1988. After completing his Jesuit training, he was ordained a priest in 1999. Father Martin's writing has appeared in a variety of newspapers and magazines, and he is the author or editor of a number of books, including two memoirs, *In Good Company: The Fast Track from the Corporate World to Poverty, Chastity, and Obedience* (Sheed & Ward, 2000) and *This Our Exile: A Spiritual Journey with the Refugees of East Africa* (Orbis, 1999). His most recent book is an edited collection entitled *Awake My Soul: Contemporary Catholics on Traditional Devotions* (Loyola Press, 2004).

A Special Invitation:

Loyola Press invites you to become one of our Loyola Press Advisors! Join our unique online community of people willing to share with us their thoughts and ideas about Catholic life and faith. By sharing your perspective, you will help us improve our books and serve the greater Catholic community.

From time to time, registered advisors are invited to participate in online surveys and discussion groups. Most surveys will take less than ten minutes to complete. Loyola Press will recognize your time and efforts with gift certificates and prizes. Your personal information will be held in strict confidence. Your participation will be for research purposes only, and at no time will we try to sell you anything.

Please consider this opportunity to help Loyola Press improve our products and better serve you and the Catholic community. To learn more or to join, visit **www.SpiritedTalk.org** and register today.

—*The Loyola Press Advisory Team*